Previously Published Wellek Library Lectures

Postcolonial Melancholia

The Wellek Lectures

Postcolonial Melancholia

Paul Gilroy

Columbia University Press New York

Columbia University Press
Publishers Since 1893
New York   Chichester, West Sussex
Copyright © 2005 Paul Gilroy

Library of Congress Cataloging-in-Publication Data
Gilroy, Paul.
     Postcolonial melancholia / Paul Gilroy.
        p. cm. — (Wellek library lectures)
     Includes bibliographical references and index.
     ISBN 0–231–13454–1 (cloth : alk. paper)
     1. Pluralism (Social sciences)—Great Britain.
     2. Race discrimination—Great Britain. 3. Minorities—
     Great Britain. 4. National characteristics, British.
     I. Title. II. Wellek Library lectures at the University of
     California, Irvine.

HM1271.G54   2004
305.8'00941—dc22   2004052692

Columbia University Press books are printed on
permanent and durable acid-free paper.

Printed in the United States of America

c 10 9 8 7 6 5 4 3 2 1

For Marcus and Cora
and in memory of Rachel Corrie and Thomas Hurndall

Editorial Note

The Wellek Library Lectures in Critical Theory are given annually at the University of California, Irvine, under the auspices of the Critical Theory Institute. The following lectures were given in May 2002.

The Critical Theory Institute
James Ferguson, Director

Contents

I'm waiting for the traffic lights to change
Waiting not to be asked for change
Waiting for this country to change

—*MC Pitman, "Waiting"*

Preface

There was a depressing and deeply symptomatic counterreaction against
the publication of The Future of Multi-Ethnic Britain: The Parekh Report
in 2000. The Blair government's indignation was directed at what it saw
as the report's unpalatable suggestion that the language and symbols of
Englishness and Britishness had a tacit racial connotation which made
them exclusionary and synonymous with whiteness. Observing that
parochial pseudo-debate unfold from a liberating distance, I was amused
and surprised to discover that, while I had not made it into the index, the
report's peculiarly controversial view had been warranted by a citation to
some earlier work of mine. The report's tepid proposition had proved

more contentious than its authors could reasonably have anticipated. Perplexed by how their obvious suggestion had aroused such scorn, I turned to a related problem: What did the reaction against it reveal about the state of the country as it struggled to come to terms with the disturbing official diagnosis of its institutional racism provided by Sir Stephen MacPherson's report on the murder of Stephen Lawrence?

It's impossible to know whether the Labour Home Secretaries, Straw and Blunkett, had noticed the perennially troublesome crowd at England football matches humming the theme tune from," *The Dambusters*, a definitive World War II film produced to elevate the national mood between Korea and Suez that reemerged at the century's end as a postmodern encomium to British pluck, steel, and eccentricity. We can only imagine what our modernizing leaders must have felt when they spotted the same fans acting out the motions of bombers swooping in on Germany to deliver their deadly World War II payloads. Why was this postwar crowd so drawn to the iconic figure of Richard Todd, in the role of Wing Commander Guy Gibson, with his faithful dog "Nigger" at heel, readying the heroes of 617 squadron to go and bomb "the Gerries." I wondered if the tribunes of New Labour squirmed as I did at the choice of that overloaded word, "nigger," as the bombers' code word for a successful strike on the Nazi dam—and if they could see that the renewed popularity of that famous film might itself point to problems with the culture of late-twentieth-century British nationalism. Baffled by their indifference to these issues, I decided to write another book about England in the hope that it might shed some light on these controversies and perhaps endow them with elements of a cosmopolitan history that they manifestly lacked. I thought this was a project that might even be enhanced by a measure of distance from the frustrations of living in the old country.

The validity of the exercise was confirmed when the New York towers fell and Blair's belligerent, sanctified, and resolutely Churchillian Britain was aligned politically with the worst and most backward features of the latest U.S. imperial adventure. Even after that low ebb, half the country's yearning to be a different kind of place seemed worth noting, pausing over, and thinking with. A new set of issues had emerged to prompt the remaking of the nation's relationship with its imperial past and to feed the hope that its buried and disavowed colonial history might become useful at last as a guide to the evasive, multicultural future prefigured everywhere in the ordinary experiences of contact, cooperation, and conflict across the supposedly impermeable boundaries of race, culture, identity, and ethnicity.

As I came to the end of the project during the summer of 2003, several British newspapers were unexpectedly occupied by the tragic plight of

Ingrid Nicholls. This forty-six-year-old black, British mum was a prospective amputee. She was catapulted up the news agenda because of a second injury that compounded the trauma involved in being told that she was about to lose her leg as a result of damage originally sustained during childhood. The additional hurt derived from the prospect of either being fitted with a pink, prosthetic limb that did not match the rest of her body or of having to find £3,000 to pay for a brown one as a private patient outside the operations of the National Health Service. Instead of a matching artificial leg, her local Health Authority had offered her counseling.

The Health Authority said that it lacked sufficient resources to fund the provision of matching prostheses to its black patients. Her conflict with it caught the nation's attention immediately and provided a measure of the country's racial temperature a decade after the Lawrence murder. Without anything being said openly, Mrs. Nicholls' experience was projected as a powerful symbol of the difficulties involved in nurturing a multicultural society and adapting its fading welfare state to the diverse needs of a multiracial patient body. However, Mrs. Nicholls' plight resonated strongly because it suggested a larger and more painful adaptation: the gradual transformation of Britain's ailing body politic in response to the demands of a black settler population whose contested right to belong was increasingly being seen as incontrovertible. One measure of that great change lay in the way the shameful refusal of a matching limb was described as an affront to her dignity. The story of these injuries seemed to be of a different order than the traditional melancholic fare: racist murder, the criminalization of the black community, and the misdeeds of white-supremacist police officers that were occasionally captured, but much more usually missed, by the hidden cameras. This was not the usual story. It was not another sad instance in which the truths of racial division and hierarchy, already known and absolutely familiar but always denied and forgotten, burst out into the light to trigger shock, disgust, and a new bout of emotional self-flagellation.

It is hard to imagine any other place where a double tale like this one—of racial difference being recognized and human dignity simultaneously denied—would have commanded such wide popular attention. Britain is used to sensationalist coverage of the natural limits to race. Its tabloids regularly cover fertility-clinic mix ups and the unanticipated arrivals of phenotypically dissimilar twins in mixed, urban families. But the image of Mrs. Nicholls, who, it was repeatedly emphasized, was "British-born" and of "mixed race," was seized upon and, I suspect, read differently. Her story became an oblique comment upon the ways in which racism has been institutionalized in British social life and a cipher for the possibility that the hurt and injury wrought by racism might be acknowledged and reversed. There was a strong sense that the unnecessary and hurtful injury to her feelings could be recognized and then remedied. Of course, like the previous year's tale of meek bureaucratic deferral to the racist wishes of donors who had been allowed to specify the racial types to which their organs could be given, this latest injury was a tragedy that should never have happened. It could not be denied and appeared to have been put right, but that was not the end of the matter. A small but significant public act of reparation was turned spontaneously into an informal act of anti-racist pedagogy. Britain was rightly ashamed but on this occasion did not turn guiltily away from the source of its discomfort. Instead, it seemed to embrace Mrs. Nicholls, who, it turned out, might not, as a result of the fuss she had made, have to lose her leg after all. Of course, it helped that Mrs. Nicholls had not brought her misfortunes upon herself. She was not a stranger, a refugee, or an asylum-seeker. The insensitive treatment meted out to her was instantly accepted as a problem with human dimensions perhaps because it did not seem to contribute directly to policy debates over "institutional racism." That too was a measure of significant change. Even while the country's hugely disproportionate black prison population grew and the total of suspicious deaths in custody kept on mounting, here was one tiny but authentic measure of a more organic and welcome modernization than the things the New Labourites have in mind as measures of our progress. In a small way, it confirmed my sense that Britain should try to make more of the conspicuous gains brought about in its civil society by an unkempt, unruly, and unplanned multiculture.

If this book anticipated Mrs. Nicholls' epiphany, it also represents the flowering of my ambivalent love of England, something that I accept as a peculiar generational and historical affliction. It addresses the mixed feelings of attachment, despair, and hope condensed in the representation of her case. The lectures on which the book was based grew in a chosen exile and were shaped by long New England winters as well as many brief, painful, and exhilarating journeys back to the homeland that I was never sure I had had. The arguments below were refined by the digital crackle of Radio 4 and Five Live heard over the Internet, by *Private Eye* and *The Observer* delivered a few days late, and by disruptive snatches of real news twisted into new meanings by being played out-of-synch with local clocks.

Postcolonial Melancholia has been made in a dense dialogue with the work of Nitin Sawhney, Mike Skinner, Rico, M. J. Cole, Pitman, Dynamite, Fallacy, Dennis Bovell, Norman Jay MBE, Rebel MC, Eliza Carthy, Martin Carthy, and many, many other outernational celebrants of the ordinary multiculturalism that distinguishes us and orients our hopes for a better country. It considers the plight of beleaguered multiculture and defends it against the accusation of failure. The discourse of human rights is then examined from the vantage point of race politics. Then the argument turns toward the issues of cosmopolitan solidarity and moral agency, which are today condemned by cheap antihumanism and vacuous identity politics alike. The latter part of the book changes direction once again to explore aspects of Britain's spontaneous, convivial culture and to discover a new value in its ability to live with alterity without becoming anxious, fearful, or violent.

I should introduce a few concepts that are fundamental to the argument below. First is the idea of "conviviality." I use this to refer to the processes of cohabitation and interaction that have made multiculture an ordinary feature of social life in Britain's urban areas and in postcolonial cities elsewhere. I hope an interest in the workings of conviviality will take off from the point where "multiculturalism" broke down. It does not describe the absence of racism or the triumph of tolerance. Instead, it suggests a different setting for their empty, interpersonal rituals, which, I suggest, have started to mean different things in the absence of any strong belief in absolute or integral races. Conviviality has another virtue that makes it attractive to me and useful to this project. It introduces a measure of distance from the pivotal term "identity," which has proved to be such an ambiguous resource in the analysis of race, ethnicity, and politics. The radical openness that brings conviviality alive makes a nonsense of closed, fixed, and reified identity and turns attention toward the always unpredictable mechanisms of identification. The book falls in two parts, loosely speaking; they are supposed to reflect a tension between cosmos and polis, global and local, worldly and parochial angles of vision. If conviviality helps to fix that primary local pole of this interpretative exercise, the other extreme can be approached via the idea of "planetarity." I have opted for this concept rather than the more familiar notion of "globalization" because those regularly confused terms, "planetary" and "global"—which do point to some of the same varieties of social phenomena—resonate quite differently. The planetary suggests both contingency and movement. It specifies a smaller scale than the global, which transmits all the triumphalism and complacency of ever-expanding imperial universals.

I hope these conceptual choices do not appear eccentric. They are important to the overall tone and direction of argument that follows because they help to precipitate a different sense of the human. The unabashed humanism that informs my argument is transgressively licensed by a critique of racial hierarchy and the infrahuman life forms it creates. I use a sense of the human that is derived from an explicit moral and political opposition *counterliberal humanism* (handwritten note in margin)

to racism in order to project a different humanity, capable of interrupting the liberal, Cold War, and exclusionary humanisms that characterize most human-rights talk. In the end, I suppose I should say that the movement aimed at extending and consolidating human rights would be stronger and far more plausible if it could show that racism was something it had thought about as a historical problem and as a corrosive feature of contemporary democracy.

Postcolonial Melancholia

Multicultural society seems to have been abandoned at birth. Judged unviable and left to fend for itself, its death by neglect is being loudly proclaimed on all sides. The corpse is now being laid to rest amid the multiple anxieties of the "war on terror." The murderous culprits responsible for its demise are institutional indifference and political resentment. They have been fed by the destruction of welfare states and the evacuation of public good, by privatization and marketization. The resurgent imperial power of the United States has made multiculturalism an aspect of the clash of integral and incompatible civilizations, thereby transmitting an additional negative energy into this delicate postcolonial process. Across *to this a post colonial present* (handwritten margin note)

Europe, parties that express popular opposition to immigration have triumphed at the polls. Xenophobia and nationalism are thriving. In Britain, difficulties arising from what is now seen as the unrealistic or unwelcome obligation to dwell peaceably with aliens and strangers somehow confirm the justice of these sorry developments. It now appears as though any desire to combine cultural diversity with a hospitable civic order (one that might, for example, be prepared to translate its own local terms into other languages or see immigration as a potential asset rather than an obvious defeat) must be subjected to ridicule and abuse.

Of course, the briefest look around confirms that multicultural society has not actually expired. The noisy announcement of its demise is itself a political gesture, an act of wishful thinking. It is aimed at abolishing any ambition toward plurality and at consolidating the growing sense that it is now illegitimate to believe that multiculture can and should be orchestrated by government in the public interest. In these circumstances, diversity becomes a dangerous feature of society. It brings only weakness, chaos, and confusion. Because unanimity is the best source of necessary strength and solidarity, it is homogeneity rather than diversity that provides the new rule.

Rather than lament the end of the various initiatives that have discredited the wholesome dream of multicultural society and reduced it to the dry dogma of a ready-mixed multiculturalism, this book offers an unorthodox defense of this twentieth-century utopia of tolerance, peace, and mutual regard.[1] Toward that end, I argue that the political conflicts which characterize multicultural societies can take on a very different aspect if they are understood to exist firmly in a context supplied by imperial and colonial history. Though that history remains marginal and largely unacknowledged, surfacing only in the service of nostalgia and melancholia, it represents a store of unlikely connections and complex interpretative resources. The imperial and colonial past continues to shape political life in the overdeveloped-but-no-longer-imperial countries.

colonial past continues to shape present (handwritten margin note)

The argument that follows warns against the revisionist accounts of imperial and colonial life that have proliferated in recent years.[2] These popular works may salve the national conscience, but they compound the marginality of colonial history, spurn its substantive lessons, and obstruct the development of multiculturalism by making the formative experience of empire less profound and less potent in shaping the life of colonizing powers than it actually was. This popular, revisionist output is misleading and dangerous because it feeds the illusion that Britain has been or can be disconnected from its imperial past. The proponents of this view rightly appreciate that a new form of colonial domination is being instituted as part of a heavily militarized globalization process. They are correct also in seeing that familiarity with the conduct of European empires has much to teach the contemporary theorists of imperial geopolitics. However, they are wrong both when they fail to recognize that the ambiguities and defects of past colonial relations persist and when they fail to appreciate that those enduring consequences of empire can be implicated in creating and amplifying many current problems. Indeed, the evasive meanings of colonial history and its potential value to the multiculturalism of the future are pending inside the new global role of the United States as successor to the European empires that were defeated and transformed during the twentieth century. It is all the more worrying that when colonial history and memory do manage to interrupt the trancelike moods of contemporary consumer culture, they have usually been whitewashed in order to promote imperialist nostalgia[3] or sanctified so that they endorse the novel forms of colonial rule currently being enforced by the economic and military means at the disposal of a unipolar global order.

These deluded patterns of historical reflection and self-understanding are not natural, automatic, or necessarily beneficial to either rulers or ruled. Instead of reinflating imperial myths and instrumentalizing imperial history, I contend that frank exposure to the grim and brutal details of my country's colonial past should be made useful: first, in shaping the character of its emergent multicultural relations, and second, beyond its borders, by being set to work as an explicit challenge to the revised conceptions of sovereignty that have been invented to accommodate the dreams of the new imperial order.[4] The revisionist ways of approaching nationality, power, law, and the history of imperial domination are, of course, fully compatible with the novel geopolitical rules elaborated after September 11, 2001. They have also been designed to conform to the economic machinery of weightless capitalism and work best when the substance of colonial history and the wounds of imperial domination have been mystified or, better still, forgotten.

As the postcolonial and post–Cold War model of global authority takes shape and reconfigures relationships between the overdeveloped, the developing, and the developmentally arrested worlds, it is important to ask what critical perspectives might nurture the ability and the desire to live with difference on an increasingly divided but also convergent planet? We need to know what sorts of insight and reflection might actually help increasingly differentiated societies and anxious individuals to cope successfully with the challenges involved in dwelling comfortably in proximity to the unfamiliar without becoming fearful and hostile. We need to consider whether the scale upon which sameness and difference are calculated might be altered productively so that the strangeness of strangers goes out of focus and other dimensions of a basic sameness can be acknowledged and made significant. We also need to consider how a deliberate engagement with the twentieth century's histories of suffering might furnish resources for the peaceful accommodation of otherness in relation to fundamental commonality. In particular, we need to ask how an increased familiarity with the bloodstained workings of racism—and the distinctive achievements of the colonial governments it inspired and legitimated— might be made to yield lessons that could be applied more generally, in the demanding contemporary settings of multicultural social relations. This possibility should not imply the exaltation of victimage or the world-historic ranking of injustices that always seem to remain the unique property of their victims. Instead of those easy choices, I will suggest that multicultural ethics and politics could be premised upon an agonistic, planetary humanism capable of comprehending the universality of our elemental vulnerability to the wrongs we visit upon each other.

In the past, western modernity described these utopian ambitions as cosmopolitan. Until recently, no shame would have automatically been attached to the simple ideals from which they derive, namely that human beings are ordinarily far more alike than they are unalike, that most of the time we can communicate with each other, and that the recognition of mutual worth, dignity, and essential similarity imposes restrictions on how we can behave if we wish to act justly. These currently rather unfashionable notions can be shown to belong to patterns of conversation and reflection that are traceable back into the dimmest historical recesses from which modern consciousness emerged. As far as the importance of empire to the modern period goes, we should remember that these ideas were entangled with and tested by the expansion of Europeans into new territories and compromised, if not wholly discredited, by the consolidation and management of the resulting imperial orders. Turned into thin ethical precepts, these insights were tried again and found wanting, most severely, by the genocidal barbarities and biopolitical atrocities of the twentieth century.

Today, any open stance toward otherness appears old-fashioned, new-agey, and quaintly ethnocentric. We have been made acutely aware of the limitations placed upon the twentieth century's cosmopolitan hopes by the inability to conceptualize multicultural and postcolonial relations as anything other than risk and jeopardy. The same aspirations have also been confounded by the problems involved in producing a worldly vision that is not simply one more imperialistic particularism dressed up in seductive universal garb.

It is more fruitful to interpret the easy refusal of cosmopolitan and humanistic desires as a failure of political imagination. That lapse is closely associated with the defeat of the Left and the retreat of the dissenting social movements with which its fate was intertwined. Those movements pursued forms of internationalism that went beyond any simple commitment to the interlocking system of national states and markets. Socialism and Feminism, for example, came into conflict with a merely national focus because they understood political solidarity to require translocal connections. In order for those movements to *move*, they had to break down the obviousness of the national state as a principle of political culture. In the process, they fostered a degree of disaffection from those who were close by but whose economic and political interests were at odds with their own. This estrangement was boldly articulated in both outlooks. Neither women nor workers were committed to a country. They turned away from the patriotism of national states because they had found larger loyalties. Their task was to fashion new networks of interconnectedness and solidarity that could resonate across boundaries, reach across distances, and evade other cultural and economic obstacles. That hope has faded away in the era of actually existing internationalism which has perversely created a political environment where cosmopolitan and translocal affiliations became suspect and are now virtually unthinkable outside of the limited codes of human-rights talk, medical emergency, and environmental catastrophe.

These restrictions on solidarity can be connected to a sense that the human sciences have become complacent, if they have not been actually undone by their reluctance to be made over as critical sciences of inhumanity. It is also linked to the limitations of philosophical anthropology as a vehicle for ethical and political reflection and to the wider constraints of a difficult moment in which, as I have said, the desire to dwell convivially with difference can appear naïve, trifling, or misplaced in the face of deepening global inequalities and conflicts over resources, on one side, and a routine, almost banal multiculture on the other.

All of these difficulties can be examined through the refusal to consider the politics of race that colors all of them. Neither humanism nor antihumanism have been comfortable or enthusiastic when asked to address the destructive impact of race thinking and racial hierarchy upon their own ways of understanding history and society. The problems have multiplied where the idea of culture has been abused by being simplified, instrumentalized, or trivialized, and particularly through being coupled with notions of identity and belonging that are overly fixed or too easily naturalized as exclusively national phenomena. Recalibrating approaches to culture and identity so that they are less easily reified and consequently less amenable to these misappropriations seems a worthwhile short-term ambition that is compatible with the long-term aims of a reworked and politicized multiculturalism. Indeed, it is doubly welcome because it requires the renunciation of the cheap appeals to absolute national and ethnic difference that are currently fashionable.

The habitual resort to culture as unbridgeable division needs to be interpreted with care. It has often been a defensive gesture, employed by minorities and majorities alike when they wrongly imagine that the hollow certainties of "race" and ethnicity can provide a unique protection against various postmodern assaults on the coherence and integrity of the self. It seems we are now condemned to work upon ourselves in conformity with the iron laws of mechanical culture just to hold our imperiled and perennially unstable identities together. In that setting, racial difference and racial hierarchy can be made to appear with seeming spontaneity as a stabilizing force. They can supply vivid natural means to lock an increasingly inhospitable and lonely social world in place and to secure one's own position in turbulent environments. Acceptance that race, nationality, and ethnicity are invariant, relieves the anxieties that arise with a loss of certainty as to who one is and where one fits. The messy complexity of social life is thereby recast as a Manichaean fantasy in which bodies are only ordered and predictable units that obey the rules of a deep cultural biology scripted nowadays in the inaccessible interiority of the genome. The logics of nature and culture have converged, and it is above all the power of race that ensures they speak in the same deterministic tongue.

Using Race to Rethink Power and Politics

Race had been essential in the elaboration of nineteenth-century political anatomy. As the concept became properly scientific, it remained an important aspect of European geopolitics in the transition toward a global predominance that was bolstered and legitimated by the transformative application of Darwin's insights. The evident reluctance of twentieth-century social thought to consider racism as more or less than ideology in general or to see race as anything other than a straightforward effect of a natural "struggle for existence" are extensions of an older pattern in which convenient assumptions about progress, nationality, and survival were overdetermined by and made congruent with various forms of racial theory.

These problems were not left behind when Europe's empires were overthrown or faded away. The racial aspects of Fascist ideology and the wars against colonial powers directed attention back toward racism. The freedom struggles of African Americans made it an urgent matter. Interest cooled as those conflicts subsided, and at that point, would-be practitioners of historical ontology became wary of both race and racism. Most opted to pursue their radical critiques of power and identity in calmer waters, usually where the creation of gender and sexual differences could be explored safely without trespassing on the political sensibilities of racial and ethnic minorities who did not appreciate their particularity being deconstructed and made to appear absurd. That development can also be seen more skeptically. Critical reflections were easiest when the elaboration of cheap antihumanist positions was unlikely to be disrupted by any inconvenient clamor from the vulnerable groups whose rights had become entangled with demands for recognition as human beings in an unjust world that denied them even that protection.

The antagonistic approach to identity pioneered by Michel Foucault could not accept that the appearance of a political language of race and its growing relationship to the administration and reproduction of governmental power were incidental developments. These were not mere coincidences in which the language of that power was momentarily addressed to the pragmatic challenges of colonial rule. Instead, the historical currency of race thinking and its tight grip on a world of empires could be used in other ways. They could, for example, tell us something fundamental and useful about the potential of "individual experience" and the shifting quality of political life, about the objects of government and the nature of subjection. A historical ontology of races could be especially useful in illuminating all the manifest contradictions—legal, ethical, military—of a civilizing mission that had to conceal its own systematic brutality in order to be effective and attractive.

Affirming the geopolitical potency of race animated the restless imperial fantasies of the English-speaking union. Racial observance could conjure away the complexities of rational irrationality and conceal the founding absurdity that elevated racial difference to a metaphysical but omnipresent political and cultural value. The attachment to race enlisted and synchronized institutions, powers, and beliefs, both religious and scientific, in the service of a colonial authority, which was not to be confined to the colonies but looped back into the biopolitical administration of metropolitan spaces and populations that were charged with a novel world-historic mission. Refusing to be resigned to race promised an alternative analysis that could grasp the ways in which race worked to limit and effectively reconstitute politics. That approach would be more useful than all the economistic theories that minimize the distinctiveness of the resulting racial order and then reduce racism to the machinations of strictly economic life. This view could, counterintuitively, also show that the entities we know as races derived from the very racial discourse that appeared to be their scientific product. The special accomplishments of racial discourse could then be explored. Its irrational rationalities, elisions, and performatives could be analyzed as substantive historical problems rather than simple but enigmatic emanations pulsing out from the decisive world of biology to shape the course of history, the rhythm of culture, and the conduct of social life. In particular, we could begin to consider the role of race and ethnic absolutism in securing the modes of inclusive exclusion that betray a distinctive ordering of power and space. Giorgio Agamben suggests that this process culminates in the institutionalized exception of the camp, which has displaced the city from its traditional position in political theory and should now be recognized as the primary political institution of our anxious age.

In the resulting world of racial and ethnic common sense, it does not matter that all demands for the recognition of supposedly absolute difference presuppose extensive transcultural knowledge that would have been impossible to acquire if cultural divisions always constituted impermeable barriers to understanding. Appreciating this paradox of discrepant ontologies provides a chance to approach the problem of multiculture from a different angle and consider instead why the alibis that derive from the cheapest invocations of incommensurable otherness command such wide respect? Why should the assertions of ethnocentricity and untranslatability that are pronounced in the face of difference have become an attractive and respectable alternative to the hard but scarcely mysterious work involved in translation, principled internationalism, and cosmopolitan conviviality? Those questions touch the core of several contemporary debates over the humanity that are implicit in the discourse of human rights. Discussions of bio- and thanato-ethics appeal to them also.

I have already departed from conventional approaches to these matters by foregrounding the issue of racial divisions. Pursuing that course, I want to assume that the "race" idea is powerful precisely because it supplies a foundational understanding of natural hierarchy on which a host of other supplementary social and political conflicts have come to rely. Race remains the self-evident force of nature in society. Our being resigned to it supports enabling analogies and provides legitimation in a host of historical situations where natural difference and social division are politically, economically, and militarily mediated. Recognizing the role of race in specifying the logic of type and the nature of difference should lead us, I submit, not deeper into an engagement with "race" or racial conflict—understood as natural phenomena, immune to the effects of historical or political process—but away from "race" altogether and toward a confrontation with the enduring power of racisms. These are forms of discourse that have become endowed with distinctive capacities. Not the least of them has been the ability to articulate a rational irrationality that undermines the very best ambitions of modern democracy by repeatedly fracturing them along raciological and nationalistic lines. The moment in which Kant compromised himself by associating the figure of the "Negro" with stupidity and connecting differences in color to differences in mental capacity provides a useful symbolic marker. From that point on, race has been a cipher for the debasement of humanism and democracy.[5]

I know that to raise awkward questions about how racism and ethnic absolutism shape governmental or juridical institutions or how they can affect academic inquiries that may seem far distant from the overspecialized subfields in which histories of racial ideas and racializing discourse are usually confined is to become suspect. Academic probity and scholarly seriousness are placed under the most intense scrutiny. More than that, the very attempt to hold "racism" together as an object to be analyzed will be unacceptable to many. To dispute racial common sense by drawing attention to these thorny and embarrassing issues is to invite dismissal as a spokesman for "political correctness" or "presentism." To take racism seriously is in effect to sacrifice much of what distinguishes the academy as a special place in which contentious and heterodox arguments will be politely heard with patience and in good faith before being refuted in a public culture for which we all assume responsibility.

Illiberal responses have been provoked by the intrusion of these irreducibly political concerns with racism. This hostility should be read historically and symptomatically. Over the years, it has been implicated in the struggles of various racialized minorities against discrimination and for political liberty and human dignity. A battle over ideas and concepts has been part of the anticolonial conflicts that have challenged the geopolitical monopoly of historicity awarded to Europe and its colonial offshoots and criticized the provincial conceptions of ethics and politics that arose from approaching modernity as an exclusively European business. That approach has been contradicted by Enrique Dussel, who has offered an alternative, world-encompassing paradigm for rethinking Europe-centered modernity on a larger scale. He presents that task as the fulfillment of an ethical obligation owed by Europe to the rest of the planet.[6] These conflicts are nothing new. They were evident in philosophy, historiography, geography, and anthropology long before the twentieth century sharpened them by multiplying opportunities to do the wrong thing with impunity and redrawing the line that divided political conflicts from ethical disputes. Arguments over racial division, over who is human enough to qualify for rights and recognition, have impinged upon the formation of epistemological and ethical as well as historical and political categories. During the twentieth century, these arguments became closely connected with the complex demands for justice and freedom made by colonial peoples bent upon changing their political status by seeking liberty from and equality with those who had held dominion over them. The intellectual architects and theorists of the anticolonial movement confirmed their complicity with the modernity of their rulers when they translated the terms of their national liberation back into the very same moral economy with which Europe's colonial order had understood its own state-building adventures and imperial enterprises. That complex history of cultural symbiosis and mutual interaction is marginalized when a dismissive tone greets suggestions that understanding racism is a worthwhile political and academic concern.

Dismissals of the idea that racism and colonial history are worthy of consideration erupted with an unusual ferocity from the very core of liberal reflection in the period after the terrorist attacks of September 2001 and in subsequent discussions of their various consequences worldwide. Old, modern notions of racial difference appear to be quietly active within the calculus that assigns differential value to lives lost according to their locations and supposed racial origins or considers that some abject human bodies are more easily and appropriately humiliated, imprisoned, shackled, starved, and destroyed than others. These obvious distinctions effectively revived a colonial economy in which infrahumanity, measured against the benchmark of healthier imperial standards, diminished rights and deferred recognition. On one memorable occasion during the final decade of the twentieth century, the economic dimensions of what had become a mainstream view were inadvertently made explicit by Lawrence Summers, then chief economist at the World Bank and now president of Harvard University. In a legendary memo that was later leaked to the environmental movement, Summers explored the reasonableness of exporting pollution to the "less developed countries" of the world. His revealing views are worth quoting at length:

> I think the economic logic behind dumping a load of toxic waste in the lowest wage country is impeccable and we should face up to that. . . . I've always thought that under-populated countries in

Africa are vastly UNDER-polluted, their air quality is probably vastly inefficiently low compared to Los Angeles or Mexico City. . . . The concern over an agent that causes a one in a million change in the odds of prostate cancer is obviously going to be much higher in a country where people survive to get prostate cancer than in a country where under 5 mortality is about 200 per thousand.

The impeccable economic logic of risk society turns out to have debts to Malthusian science, which can be implemented in the "struggle for existence" understood now as a global rather than a national project. Summers' observations show how easily the eugenic fantasies of the early twentieth century can be revived and filtered into the unrecognizable residues of seventeenth-century natural-law theory, which, we should recall, had been produced originally with the needs of acquisitive North American colonists in mind.

Though Summers made no mention of racial difference, I believe that the assumptions of racial hierarchy were active in securing his combination of arguments, which contains an echo of the suggestion that the inhabitants of the less-developed countries are themselves a form of planetary pollution.[7] The natives, whose bodies are comparatively worthless, already exist in a space of death, for which their characteristic lack of industry makes them responsible. Like the generic enemies, the invisible prison inmates, and all the other shadowy "third things"[8] that race thinking lodges between animal and human, their lives are best administered under the flexible governance produced by special emergency rules and exceptional or martial laws. The lowly biopolitical status common to all these groups underscores the fact that they cannot be reciprocally endowed with the same vital humanity enjoyed by their rulers, captors, conquerors, judges, executioners, and other racial betters.

The reappearance of these sentiments under the sign of progress and globalization is an urgent matter. However, that is not what has provoked the argument that follows. The source of those complaints lies in frustrations of longer standing, induced by the fact that the political significance of racism is only acknowledged once the banners of absolute ethnicity and armored identity have been unfurled and the tableaux of differentiation are being ritually enacted. The denial, displacement, and refusal triggered by demonstrations of the efficacy of racism and racial hierarchy now have an independent impact upon the life-chances and hopes of those designated as racially inferior and therefore marginal and infrahuman. I want to suggest not only that these patterns have history and can be understood as social and political rather than natural phenomena, but to ask us to look again at where they have entered into the habits and intuitions of the human sciences, where they have corrupted the workings of government, justice, commerce, and communication. This orientation requires something more extensive than a commitment to undo institutional racism in which the production of inequalities does not depend upon any prior attachment of individual actors to racist ideology or belief. We are being drawn beyond that necessary but insufficient stance into a view of racial discourse as endowed with its own political life and institutional tempo. It generates a field of ethics, knowledge, and power that contributes its unique order of truths to the processes that produce and regulate individual subjects, conditioning the intimate consciousness through which they come to know and understand and indeed constitute themselves as racial beings.

The Right to Be Human

The disinclination to address these dynamics has now become a significant problem. It has entered directly into the life of postcolonial Europe in a number of ways. In the case of Britain, which I will address in more detail later on, a refusal to think about racism as something that structures the life of the postimperial polity is associated with what has become a morbid fixation with the fluctuating substance of national culture and identity. In a revealing pattern established by Winston Churchill's influential triangulation of the post-1945 world, the core of British particularity is deemed to be under disastrous attack from three different directions: Americanization, Europeanization, and a nonspecific subsumption by immigrants, settlers, and invaders of both colonial and postcolonial varieties. Behind these multiple anxieties lies the great transformation that quickly reduced the world's preeminent power to a political and economic operation of more modest dimensions. We must become interested in how the literary and cultural as well as governmental dynamics of the country have responded to that process of change and what it can tell us about the place of racism in contemporary political culture.

Strong resistance against the idea that racism can shape historical and cultural relationships has come from across the spectrum of respectable political opinion. This sort of response is not, of course, confined to Britain. The suggestion that racism can exist significantly and perniciously in unconscious and supraindividual forms and that critical analysis of its potency can contribute something to the life of the humanities and the quality of broader civic interaction is also widely rejected. Advocacy of the idea that there is a political or ethical obligation to deal with racism and its consequences has been dismissed as an endorsement of victimology, as special pleading, or as an implicit rejection of universal and liberal standards of justice and governance. Governmental concessions to antiracism policies made in response to minority demands are queried or rejected on the grounds that they are unfair or unjust. This outcome feeds another category of objection. It says that even if racism is sometimes pernicious and occasionally endowed with the capacity to debase the finest coinage of political culture, identifying it as a specific object of governmental intervention can only multiply the problems. If racism and its social consequences are regrettable, answering them politically or juridically is, according to this influential position, doomed to be counterproductive. Racism's deindividualizing effects can be adequately countered with large doses of individualism, its antidemocratic results repudiated with infusions of a generic democratic energy that need not or rather should not be made specific. Michael Ignatieff has been a distinguished and forthright spokesman for this point of view. He says, bluntly dismissing the strategies against institutional racism proposed to the British government by Sir William Macpherson in 1999 that "if racism is in the eye of the beholder, we will never be finished with it. . . . We do not need to police each other's thoughts and attitudes toward our differences."9 At a stroke, the political and judicial voices raised bravely during the preceding decades in order to identify the corrosive operations of racism in the workings of polity and economy have been repudiated. In a different historical setting that requires a more muted tone, he dismisses the idea that there could be any form of systematic reparation for the consequences of racial slavery and territorial expropriation in the Atlantic world:

> The problem is that the majority has genuine difficulty accepting the idea that present generations remain responsible for the harms committed by past ones. How long must the Canadian majority continue to pay for the abuses done to aboriginal peoples in times past? How long must it do penance for racism, sexism and other forms of injustice? . . . The victim minorities resent depending on the majority for redress. The majority resents depending on the minority for forgiveness. Since forgiveness would foreclose future claims, victims tend to withhold it; since redress implies culpability, it too is withheld. So the politics of argument is replaced by a politics of blackmail and stonewalling.10

These words resonate far beyond the Canadian case. Indeed similar patterns of denial, tacit hostility, and essential indifference to the claims for restitution can be discovered in many areas of the globe where the shadows of racial slavery and other varieties of brutal colonial domination linger on. I hope to show that the desire for redress can involve more than a "politics of blackmail," which is not, as Ignatieff well knows, any kind of politics at all. As far as Britain is concerned, the need to find an answer to these smooth arguments is urgent and requires more than a sociological explanation. In Britain these arguments are tied to an obsessive repetition of key themes—invasion, war, contamination, loss of identity—and the resulting mixture suggests that an anxious, melancholic mood has become part of the cultural infrastructure of the place, an immovable ontological counterpart to the nation-defining ramparts of the white cliffs of Dover.

In seeking an explanation for the widespread reluctance to engage racism analytically, historically, or governmentally, we may observe charitably that questions about "race," identity, and differentiation have a distinctive, mid-twentieth century ring to them. They sometimes feel anachronistic because they do try to return contemporary discussion to a moral ground that we feel we should have left behind long ago. Many people are inclined to be impatient about being asked to revisit aspects of the political and moral debate over "race" that followed the defeat of the Third Reich and flowered with the reflection on racial difference, history, and culture that was triggered by UNESCO's midcentury initiatives against racism. That return is necessary because consideration of these questions has only a minimal presence in today's incomplete genealogies of the global movement for human rights, which are inclined to imagine that conflict between "race" and more inclusive models of humanity was concluded long ago. If the historical anomaly represented by archaic racial division does, contrary to expectations, remain legally or morally open, if it is still somewhere "on hold" and therefore a muted part of the history of our present, the discomforting events to which these discussions refer are most likely to be recovered or remembered in the name of the same racial, ethnic, and national absolutes and particularities that I intend to call into question. "Race" would then become an eternal cause of racism rather than what it is for me—its complex, unstable product. I should probably emphasize at this point that neither race nor racism are the exclusive historical property of the minorities who are their primary victims.

With these conceptual dangers in mind, it is probably better from the start to face up to the fact that the variety of inquiry proposed here harks back to the immediate context of the United Nations "Universal Declaration," which was adopted by the UN General Assembly on 10 December 1948. The dissonant notes of that document resounded in a political setting shaped not only by the aftermath of conflict with Fascism but by the colonial warfare that attended the independence of twenty-five African countries between 1956 and 1962. This period saw western powers resisting decolonization militarily in Algeria, Indonesia, Malaya, Aden, Madagascar, and Indochina. For the purposes of what follows, this moment can productively be triangulated by the foundation of South Africa's Apartheid state, by the establishment of the state of Israel in Palestine as a novel historical experiment in both nation building and colonization as reparation, and by the partition of India. All of these events are linked directly to the history and decomposition of the British Empire. All involved the deployment of separatist political technologies, and all of them speak to the currency and limits of racialized governance with great power because the shadow cast over politics and government by the Third Reich was so profound.

A planetary debate over "race" and racism emerged from this phase of nation building and geopolitical realignment. It had to address the issue of racial difference between societies as well as the violent eruption of readily racialized cultural and ethnic conflicts within them. It bears repetition that a special moral impulse was drawn from the defeat of Fascism. Racism was presented as a problem of civilization with implications for the development of humanity as a whole.[11] The segmentation of the human species that resulted from pathological attachments to "race" was firmly identified with genocide and catastrophe. This moment demanded a complete political and philosophical response to race lore that could supplement the historical understanding of the checkered career of "race" as a contested scientific concept.

Writing during the late 1940s, Hannah Arendt and Jean-Paul Sartre addressed these problems in different ways. Their responses to the challenge of that special moment provide the implicit backdrop to the historical opportunity I want to identify. Arendt went to great lengths to distinguish racism from nationalism, arguing that it needed to be addressed as a specific problem of politics that arose from colonial conquest and rule. She renamed Nazism "race imperialism" and was certain that the characteristic brutality of European colonial rule was one of the most important "elements which crystallized into totalitarianism." We should recall that her explanation of how racism developed began with a discussion of South Africa, where the Boer settlers at the Cape were the original architects of a ruthless and practical racism that would supply new social and political rules for colonial organization elsewhere. The routine application of what would eventually become known as the doctrine of preemption might, for example, be traced to these early colonial adventures and the forms of warfare they engendered.

Sartre proposed a "concrete liberalism" in response to the horrors that racism had recently sanctioned. It was informed by a reconstructed humanism that had been shaped by his acute sense of the inability of the colonizer's humanitarianism to accommodate the humanity of the colonized. This outlook was a guide to action. It was tailored so as to compensate for the failures that had made genocidal Nazism possible. This involved displacing the body of the victim from the center of the analysis and finding a new place for it. Here the "Jewish Problem" and the "Negro Problem" gave way to the very different problems represented by anti-Semitism and anti-black racism. It was the racist and the anti-Semite who, in effect, created the objects of their hatred. The political task of defeating racism required that attention was turned in that direction.

We will see that these philosophers' unsettling questions—aimed at comprehending the fragmentation of humankind into racial groups and preventing the recurrence of genocide—have remained with us during the intervening years. This agenda can be defined by its considerations of the singularity and uniqueness of Nazi racial politics. It was intermittently present in the atmosphere created by the human- and civil-rights struggles that transformed the civic apparatus of the United States, and it surfaced again periodically amidst campaigns to change the exclusionary structures of the colonial world. Through much of the Cold War, in opposition to national liberation struggles, the process of modern historical development was still being constructed in the distinctively racialized terms of the later nineteenth century.[12] The history of this midcentury debate over racial orders is accessible, but its growing importance demands a break with the rarified tones and ultratheoretical mode in which much contemporary discussion of multiculture, toleration, and otherness has been conducted. In other words, a renewed and much more direct confrontation with the issues of racial hierarchy and cultural diversity is now necessary.

Posing the provocative cosmopolitan questions with which I began transports us rapidly to the limits of the available analytical approaches—most of which are, as we have seen, decidedly wary of acknowledging racism as an active and dynamic political force. The timid way in which these inquiries are usually framed betrays a hesitation compounded by the fear of being denounced as "politically correct." Contemporary discussion has cooled down a lot since the midcentury eruption I have described. If it survives at all, critical reflection on racism is likely to be diverted toward two equally unsatisfactory destinations. The first can be identified through its affirmation of practical action. This is commendable in many ways but becomes suspect where enthusiasm for praxis combines with hostility toward reflection. The evasive unity of theory and practice is then replaced by the unconditional exaltation of practice, unencumbered by thought. What was racial politics becomes policy or therapy and then simply ceases to be political. At best, the enhancement of racial equality and the battle against racial injustice become technical problems to be managed and administered. The principal alternative can be represented through highly abstract considerations of tolerance, relativism, and humanism that have recently become fashionable in scholastic circles. These have seldom been registered in critical theory as anything other than the detritus of impotent or disinterested bourgeois reflection. As far as the history of race politics at home, that is, in the core of the old imperial systems where postcolonial settlers are fighting for citizenship and dignity, the silence on these questions is deafening. The post-colonial rereading of literary texts, works of art, and other objects of docile cultural history has, for the most part, not been able to find its way back to the disreputable, angry places where the political interests of racialized minorities might be identified and worked upon without being encumbered by an affected liberal innocence, on the one hand, or by the conservative spell of ethnic absolutism, on the other.

Though I value the legacy of some of these conversations, especially those which derive from the anticolonial movement's need for theories of agency that made sense of its goals and Cold War predicament, I want to pursue some different options. The tidy models of governance, legality, and power on which polite scholastic debates about racial division have relied no longer have much to contribute. Contemporary discussions of immigration, asylum, nationalism, and other areas of government where race is strongly resonant have been enriched not only by the capacity to reflect clearly on the history of decolonization but also by consideration of the conceptions of political power that resulted from detours through the bloody history of colonial societies and the planetary ambitions of race-driven imperialism. Disturbing views of government in action can be derived from close historical studies of colonial domination, to which the idea of "race" and the machinations of racial hierarchy were always integral. As Arendt so correctly identified, the understanding of the state-formation process generated by the study of colonial government contrasts with the orthodoxies that have emerged from narrower histories of Europe, conceived as a wholly innocent and essentially self-contained entity. The elaboration of this counterhistory raises another exciting possibility, namely that centering a salvage of modern democracy on the stubborn persistence and effects of racism might itself yield rich and productive redefinitions of what liberalism was and what cosmopolitan democracy will be.

Some beguiling political models assume metropolitan governance to be innocent and colonial administration to be benign. They were tailored to fit the asymmetrical contours of a divided world that was itself created and projected in racialized forms. That stratified world is now haunted by racial phantoms, fantastic figures derived from political exigencies defined at the terminal points of European trading activity. That racialized world has been subsequently populated by the unholy progeny of at least two additional layers of raciological and geopolitical theory. The first had been originally invented to rationalize the era of Europe's great colonial empires, while the second was produced more recently to affirm the very different racial order that is becoming visible now that U.S. specifications and assumptions about difference, culture, and phenotype are disseminated under the global reach of contemporary corporate powers. To cut a long story short, the first saw "The Negro" only as a sub- or infrahuman figure, while its successor has sometimes been prepared to identify the same incredible subspecies as superhuman and even godlike in its physicality. Michael Jordan and Mike Tyson, Halle Berry and the tennis-playing Williams sisters are some of the iconic presences that embody the later possibility. Of course, these grand traditions for making "race" meaningful intersect where the concept of "humanity" has itself been shaped to accommodate the fragmentation and division of racial thinking.

The political and ethical impact of this complex and internally differentiated racial humanity can be considered from a variety of perspectives. One of the more promising involves consideration of how the exclusionary principles of modern, political nationality were actively racialized by their imperial exponents in order to win novel varieties of active consent from an emergent working class that was being simultaneously civilized and recomposed in the biopolitical conditions that had fostered popular imperialist feeling. Managing imperial projects required new governmental institutions at home; it promoted a distinctive approach to the lives of all racial groups and to the ambiguous ideal of universal humanity that had been shattered by the shock of World War I. The shape of this development was captured by this comment on the prosecution of modern, industrial wars, drawn from the increasingly influential work on the constitution of political relations and conflicts that was done by the Nazi jurist Carl Schmitt. It is weighed down by his many resentments, particularly against the League of Nations and what he saw as the unproductive extraction of reparations from Germany after 1918. However, his general argument seems clear enough and may, unwittingly have provided a useful point of departure for the analysis of more recent geopolitical developments:

The concept of humanity is an especially useful ideological instrument of imperialist expansion, and in its ethical-humanitarian form it is a specific vehicle of economic imperialism . . . To confiscate the word humanity, to invoke and monopolize such a term probably has certain incalculable effects, such as denying the enemy the quality of being human and declaring him an outlaw of humanity; and a war can thereby be driven to the most extreme inhumanity.[13]

Schmitt's patriotic desire to place Germany high on the resulting list victims of this fraud and his absolute disinterest in the political mechanisms of empire and colony limit the value of this insight. It is nonetheless useful in showing where the postmodern geopolitics of today's new imperium can be mapped on to the breakdown of the colonial order and how those interrelated categories, race and humanity, have been pivotal in the transition from one to the other.

Enemy Aliens

The vexed relationship between cultural differences and the ordering principles of national states has become a huge political and juridical issue since the September 2001 attacks on the United States. Those events have been widely interpreted as part of a conflict between contending civilizations. Indeed, the Bush administration's "war on terror" might be thought of as having brought the slumbering civilizational giants of Christendom and the Orient back to life. The integrity of these homogenous, monolithic entities is simply assumed, but, in the case of the West, it is telling that even when armed to the teeth, its fortified wholeness is imperiled, subject to anxiety about the prospect of its durability and tormented by the knowledge of its inevitable decline. That realization shapes an apparently neurotic fascination with how the local and immediate political loyalties owed by citizens compare to the different obligations due from prisoners, transients, aliens, settlers, and dissidents. These insecurities have coincided with the inauguration of a bigger version of the polarizing mechanism celebrated in Schmitt's notorious definition of the political through its capacity to comprehend and activate the rather theological distinction between friend and enemy.[14] President Bush's determination to constitute a pattern of political relationships in which not being for him, his government, and, by extension, the United States, was enough to designate oneself as their enemy solidified and militarized the polity. The possibility of any loyalty more cosmopolitan than national deference was thrown into ferment.

The governmental correlates of his belligerent initiative have high-lighted the marginal and infrahuman status of noncitizens inside the EU and the United States. Unusual legal initiatives were begun as part of this new and apparently endless conflict and proved difficult to analyze because their colonial antecedents had not been made clear. The more than 600 detainees forcibly held at the U.S. government's Cuban "Camp Delta" were for more than two years denied access to legal assistance and separated from the jurisdiction of the many and various sovereign countries from which they derived their nationality or citizenship. These men were held indefinitely and without charge neither as criminals nor as prisoners of war but as "battlefield detainees" and "enemy combatants." These are obscure paralegal categories that had appeared on the fringes of battlefields before. They appeared to be useful at this juncture because they helped to populate the exceptional judicial and governmental space that accommodates infrahuman forms that are familiar from earlier formations of colonial government.

That special space is governed by rules that are much closer to martial law than to civil codes. There, the contestable issue of the prisoners' precise legal subjectivity is not allowed to arise. This is info-war, and these terrorists will not be given the platform of a public trial. Their dubious struggle will not be sustained by "the oxygen of publicity." It is worth asking what their exceptional status owed to the pragmatic precedents that had been established during colonial wars. Those conflicts were always conducted outside of the rules that had been established over a long period of time to regulate the different varieties of violence that erupted between properly civilized peoples or nations. In that honorable company, the distinction between combatants and noncombatants was more likely to be recognized, and any captured prisoners might even be treated humanely rather than summarily put to death in what amounted to spontaneous acts of racial hygiene or ethnic cleansing. It is well known that in recognition of a certain racial reciprocity, only particular types of weaponry were judged acceptable among Europeans. There were no restrictions on the creative deployment of killing technology in their different confrontations with the world's uncivilized hordes.

There have been many instances in which political conflicts that were made intelligible through racial or ethnic difference proved to have been an important factor in institutionalizing departures from the legal and moral rules that governed more wholesome wars between racial equals. These issues are especially pertinent to discussions of British colonial history. The bloody conflict over law, terror, and administrative killing that took place at Jamaica's Morant Bay in 1865 has been institutionalized as a key source of the independent island's national identity. It provides a useful illustration of these matters. The ensuing debate over legitimacy and violence in colonial administration split Britain's Victorian bourgeoisie and its intellectual substratum down the middle. The whole case is too long and complex to reconstruct in its entirety here. However, it raises a number of issues that do have a continuing significance: the colony as a place of governmental experiment and innovation, the useful or tactical ambiguities of martial law, and the systematic use of torture to obtain confessions. One particular element that was the focus of much anxiety at the time also seems pertinent to our contemporary debates. It concerns the movement of prisoners from one jurisdiction to another or even into special locations where there is no jurisdiction as such. Having surrendered himself to the authorities, George William Gordon, an important political opponent of the colony's governor, Edward Eyre, was actually transferred by boat from an area under civil law to a different location where martial rules operated. This was done precisely in order for him to be put to death with a minimum of governmental inconvenience.[15] This instrumental or permissive relationship between power and law recurs and can be considered a distinguishing feature of colonial governance. Its characteristic effects are registered in the writings of those historians who follow Leon Radzinowicz in the convenient belief that the concept of martial law is unknown to English law or who find their understanding of that law's special value to colonial administration confounded by the peculiar proposition that martial law can be simultaneously both the absence of law and its highest expression: the general entitlement of sovereign power to deploy violence in order to overcome challenges to its own authority.[16]

What this peculiarity may have contributed to the actual conduct of colonial warfare during the second half of the nineteenth century can be explored through a close reading of Colonel C. E. Callwell's classic study *Small Wars: Their Principle and Practice*. This dazzling compendium of comparative information on guerilla, unconventional, or other novel types of warfare with savages and other uncivilized people was first published in 1896. It is a voluminous text that has an additional value to historians of the postcolonial present because it was written entirely within the vocabulary and assumptions of the crudest English racial science. At first, I was puzzled by the fact that its many tactical recipes, which cover terrain, livestock, mobility, and every other aspect of the colonial sort of fighting, make no mention of the management of prisoners. I realized that prisoners were not an issue for Callwell because there was no possibility that any would be taken. His tone is typically downbeat and the argument he makes is all the more powerful for being couched in a commentary on the fate of civilized troops who fall into savage hands rather than the other way around: "in conflict with savages and semi-civilized opponents, and even in many cases with guerillas in a civilized country, there is no such thing as surrender. The fate of the force which sacrifices itself in a small war is in most cases actual destruction."[17] These rules, legal and practical, ensured that the colonial insurgent, rather like the slave in earlier phases of imperial dominance, already belonged among the socially dead. The deadly combination of indigeneity and insurgency meant that they were only awaiting the carrying out of that suspended sentence. Their extinction supplies timely proof that the modern laws of nature and history are acting as one.

The predicament of the latest captives in Cuba becomes easier to comprehend if these and other similar cases are remembered. The Camp Delta prisoners are held simultaneously inside and outside the law on the same Caribbean island that gave birth to the institution of the concentration camp in the late nineteenth century. Their plight suggests that the most fundamental lines of division are no longer those that separate citizens from stateless people. The tenure of national citizenship can now be easily revoked or diminished. It affords no more guarantees. Instead, the variety and relative geopolitical stature of contending citizenships are to be evaluated in relation to the political orientation of the civilization that issued and authorized them. That ranking operation is now a principal consideration.

Civilizationism

Old colonial issues come back into play when geopolitical conflicts are specified as a battle between homogenous civilizations arranged, as George Orwell put it lucidly in another context, as if "the world is an assemblage of sheep and goats, neatly partitioned off by national frontiers."[18] Today's civilizationism shamelessly represents the primary lines of antagonism in global politics as essentially cultural in character. Its figuration of the post–Cold War world bears the significant imprint of the grand, nineteenth-century racial theory that was formed by the terrifying prospect of racial decline and degeneracy. Gobineau's influential *Essay on the Inequality of Human Races* has a disputed place in the genealogy of modern race thinking, but in 1854, he had managed to identify ten civilizations. In the early 1990s, Samuel Huntington could locate only seven. Despite their many differences, both writers share a preoccupation with the dynamics of intercivilizational repulsion and the disastrous consequences of attempts at intermixture. Gobineau identified the ultimate danger to civilizations in any departure from "the homogeneity necessary to their life" and the consequent loss of what he calls "the common logic of existence."[19] Huntington specifies the same sort of raciological and geopolitical problem aphoristically in the contemporary idiom of multiculturalism and globality:

> Multiculturalism at home threatens the United States and the West; universalism abroad threatens the West and the world. Both deny the uniqueness of western culture. The global monoculturalists want to make the world like America. The domestic multiculturalists want to make America like the world. A multi-cultural America is impossible because a non-Western America is not American. A multicultural world is unavoidable because global empire is impossible.[20]

Unlike Gobineau, Huntington was prepared to concede the possibility of an African civilization, but his inclusion of Apartheid South Africa on his 1960 map of the free world reveals the limits of his understanding with regard to the human resources at its disposal.

It bears repetition that civilizationism requires any cosmopolitan consciousness or commitment to be ridiculed. Its dubious authority makes it impossible to imagine that local, national, and ethnic connections and loyalties do not exhaust any individual. And so it becomes unacceptable to even ask whether these ties might constitute obstacles to the operations of conscience or to moral investments. Hopes that cannot be confined within the borders of a national culture are idle wishes: castles in the air. Authoritarian modes of belonging to the national collective supply the norm, and with the constraints and strengths of national identity and the national-state system plainly visible, anyone who objects to the conduct of their government is likely to be identified as an enemy within and bluntly advised to go and live elsewhere. Attempts to criticize a national state while simultaneously living under its protective umbrella become hypocrisy rather than the principled pursuit of consistency. To make matters even worse, we are informed that the end of the national state was prematurely announced during mistaken earlier phases of globalization. We are then reminded that the principle of duty must, above all, be a national one and that our dwindling rights cannot be separated from obligations that will be defined, if we are fortunate, by an ideal of patriotic citizenship in which being for those who are like oneself does not *necessarily* mean being opposed to those whose equivalent ties and comparable affiliations lie elsewhere.

The militarization of social life promotes an automatic solidarity in which soldier-citizens who carry or practice the defining culture of their national state become indistinguishable to the point of being interchangeable. This enforced or serial solidarity was what Orwell was getting at when, in the immediate aftermath of war, he offered an expanded typology of nationalism that included both Zionism and "Colour Feeling." He described a political outlook defined initially "by the habit of assuming that human beings can be classified like insects." Acknowledging that nationalistic loves and hatreds are part of the makeup of most of us, he argued that the struggle against them required a moral effort that had to begin from "discovering what one really is, what one's own feelings really are, and then making allowance for the inevitable bias."[21] The dominance of authoritarian political formations and the orchestration of nationalistic moods set out to close down every opportunity for that variety of reflection. The info-war is already underway. It erases any possibility that dissent might have a positive value and declares that seeking any distance from the national culture's center of gravity is a form of low-grade treachery. By addressing conflicts *between* groups of associated national states rather than *within* them, civilizationist common sense scorns the idea that public dissidence could ever be a measure of the buoyancy and health of a democracy. That unpopular idea had resurfaced from the cosmopolitan hopes of the generation that, like Orwell himself, in rejecting both Fascism and Stalinism, articulated larger loyalties: to humanity and to civilization. These commitments were conceived in far more ambivalent and complex patterns than are currently fashionable. This was not simply a matter of Left against Right: Adorno's observations on the radical homelessness of the intellectual in *Minima Moralia* can be offset against Eric Auerbach's hopeful recycling of Hugo of St. Victor's prescient observation on the perfection of the man for whom "the whole world is as a foreign land."

The fundamental point is that today, cosmopolitan estrangement and democracy-enriching dissent are not prized as civic assets. They are just routine signs of subversion and degeneration. More than that, the predicted breakdown in the reproduction of appropriate national consciousness has arisen just where Gobineau, Huntington, and a host of prophetic, civilizationist voices had predicted: where the deceit of the terrorists and the catastrophic effects of mass immigration by the alien populations from which they emanate have distorted what we can call the proper cultural ecologies of national states, which we are expected to believe were homogenous until the immigrants showed up after 1945. The appearance of Europe's postcolonial citizens, caged under the Caribbean sun in

"Camp Delta," supplies new proof of the enduring value of the old national-state system, just as their diasporic dispersal and rootless transnationality provide a timely measure of its limits.

State-sponsored patriotism and ethnic-absolutism are now dominant, and nationalism has been reconstituted to fit new social and geopolitical circumstances in which the larger West and our own local part of it are again under siege. However, the work involved in knowing oneself and understanding the traditional, defining norms of one's own official culture is not as easy as it might have been in the past. Technology, deindustrialization, consumerism, loneliness, and the fracturing of family forms have changed the character and content of those ethnic and national cultures as much or even more than immigration ever did. We will see that under pressure from the leveling and homogenizing elements of cultural globalization, national identity and national consciousness have had to become objects of governmental intervention in elaborate ways. New technologies of the neonational self, particularly in the form of elaborate sporting spectacle, are a conspicuous feature of this moment, in which the appeal of sub- and supranational forms of identification has also been marked. In Britain, our sternest leaders have comforted us with a new rule that any new arrivals will henceforth by expected to learn and to adhere to traditional norms and values even though they may not be widely practiced in the country at large. It is probably significant in this context that some of the young Englishmen of Asian descent implicated in the country's rioting of summer 2001 were overheard taunting their white supremacist attackers not with racial slurs that inverted the insults hurled in the other direction but with the more provocative assertion that they, unlike their supposed racial betters, were not disposed to place their aging parents and grandparents in institutional care. One young man interviewed by the *Daily Mirror* challenged the civilizationist folklore about the sources of the conflict with an important and neglected explanation of how the hatred directed by whites against Asians had come about: " 'I'll give you an example of why they [the whites] dislike us so much,' he said, fingering a top-of-the-range Nokia mobile phone. 'It's jealousy. See, we start working young—I started helping my dad at 11—and whenever we buy anything we pay cash. At 17 we have saved enough for our first car. It might cost £2,000. A couple of years later we sell it and buy one for £5,000, and by 21 we've got a brand new BMW.' "22

The demise of socialist and Feminist movements that were committed to the observance of what might be termed an open, nonnational solidarity has also contributed to this situation, in which cultural nationalism, cheap patriotism, and absolute ethnicity supply the potent default settings for political identity and political analysis of postcolonial conflicts. The next chapter will explore how the retreat of those oppositional utopias has been coupled with the rise of a translocal human-rights movement that resolves discrepancies between diverse groups into a beautiful but also frustratingly abstract and sometimes ethnocentric understanding of the human.

Part One The Planet

1   Race and the Right to Be Human

The horrors of the twentieth century brought "races" to political life far more vividly and naturalistically than imperial conquest and colonial administration had done. Our postcolonial environment reverberates with the catastrophes that resulted from the militarized agency and unprecedented victimization of racial and ethnic groups. It is not surprising that contemporary analysis of racism and its morbidities still belongs emphatically to that unhappy period. It should be obvious that critical analysis of racisms needs to be self-consciously and deliberately updated. Few new ways of thinking "race" and its relationship to economics, politics, and power have emerged since the era of national-liberation struggles to guide the continuing pursuit of a world free of racial hierarchies.

If we are seeking to revive that goal, to make it sound less banal, more attractive, and more political by showing where it touched and still transforms modern dreams of substantive democracy and authentic justice, then we will need to reconstruct the history of "race" in modernity. That task entails offering multiple genealogies of racial discourse that can explain how the brutal, dualistic opposition between black and white became entrenched and has retained its grip on a world in which racial and ethnic identities have been nowhere near as stable or fixed as their accompanying rhetoric would have us believe.

Those worthy goals introduce a conflict between the obligation to pay attention to local and conjunctural factors and the lingering desire for a totalizing theory that can explain the attachment to "race" and ethnicity under all conditions. The former is demanded by a subversive commitment to the relocalization of a networked world; the latter is animated by the troubling fantasy of controlling that world by reducing it to a set of elegant categories. This attempt to reconcile the irreconcilable claims of the abstract and the immediate involves returning in a systematic fashion to the interpretations of racism and racial hierarchy that were produced during the Cold War, to the alternative formulations that emerged from critical theorists and national liberation struggles as well as those that flowed from the confrontation with a variety of differing incarnations of Fascism, not all of which appealed openly or consistently to the metaphysics of "race."

Along this path we will be obliged to consider the fate of left, libertarian, and cosmopolitan thought during the twentieth century and to ask why there have been so few successor projects capable of articulating antiracist hope in anything other than its negative moment: that is, as a creative conjuring with the possibility of better worlds rather than embattled criticism of this comprehensively disenchanted one.

Though they were addressed to a very different context, Adorno's challenging words on the relationship between nationality, ethnicity, and forms of intellectual freedom can usefully be borrowed here. They communicate something of the problem that arises from dissenting contemplation of the mystified, alienated arrangement to which racial truths and biocultural ontologies have supplied indices of realness and provided key markers in the formation of sensible social policy, mature political thought, and good scholarly habits. This is how Adorno described the relationship between critical theory and the racialization of knowledge itself: "The person who interprets instead of accepting what is given and classifying it is marked with the yellow star of one who squanders his intelligence in impotent speculation, reading things in where there is nothing to interpret."[1] Transposed into our project, his observation points to the way in which racial politics has been obstructively invested with common sense. His words underline that the signs of "race" do not speak for themselves and highlight the fact that the difficult work of interpreting the system of meaning they create is always likely to appear illegitimate, "politically incorrect," sometimes treasonable and usually speculative in the most dismissive sense of that term. Adorno also reminds us that, while the political order of "race" endures, the character of racial and ethnic groups is seen to be at stake in attempts to overthrow it. Racism involves a mode of exploitation and domination that is not merely compatible with the phenomena of racialized differences but has amplified and projected them in order to remain intelligible, habitable, and productive.

Race thinking and the distinctive political forms associated with it—biopower, ultranationalism, ethnic absolutism, and so on—have sanctioned gross brutality in many diverse settings. Social and political theory have been reluctant to address this recurrence. It is not usually seen as a specific interpretative, historical, or ethical problem; it is never approached as a result of what Frantz Fanon described as the "delerium" of race-friendly Manichaeism. It is more likely that this pattern is used to focus on very different matters: the question of a universal predisposition to evil or the convenient image of a never-ending conflict between civilization and savagery.

We are now in a position to understand that the raciology that has made this repetition possible is a result of modern political culture with special ties to its philosophies of power, government, and statecraft. Rather than simply compiling an inventory of catastrophic episodes in which the power of "race" or ethnicity has been made manifest, I think we should be prepared to explore the moral and conceptual challenges that those systems of thought place before us. In a sense, then, taking not the idea of "race" but the power of racisms more seriously means accepting that there may be a degree of tension between the professional obligations to recover and to remain faithful to the past and the moral and political imperative to act against the injustices of racial hierarchy as we encounter them today.

The spirit in which we undertake this work is therefore critical, and, whether we like it or not, recognizing the power of racism makes us historians of the present with all the special responsibilities that entails. We must, for example, be especially careful not to project contemporary dynamics backward into circumstances with which they cannot possibly be congruent, nor should we imagine the world always to have been as starkly black and white as it sometimes looks these days. In this transitional period, we must deal with the fact that to engage racism seriously involves moving simultaneously onto historical and political ground. It cannot be otherwise. The urgency of this moment leaves no room for disinterested or inert contemplation of racial hierarchy and its injustices.

When the idea of "race" becomes a concept, it poses clear and incompatible alternatives. Once we comprehend racism's alchemical power, we do have to choose. We can opt to reproduce the obligations of racial observance, negotiating them but basically accepting the idea of racial hierarchy and then, inescapably, reifying it. Or there is a second and far more difficult and rewarding alternative, in which for clearly defined moral and perhaps political reasons we try to break its spell and to detonate the historic lore that brings the virtual realities of "race" to such dismal and destructive life. This dilemma is acute because racist discourses have so often entailed strict rules about the historical character of the hierarchies they create. As Eric Wolf and countless others have shown, the acquisition of unassailable human status with all its subjective, judicial, and political benefits, has regularly involved arguments about the geo- and biopolitical boundaries of national states and the cultural character of the historical processes that support their existence. To be recognized as human was to be accorded an authentic kind of historic being. On the other hand, to be dismissed on raciological grounds as bestial or infrahuman was to be cast outside of both culture and historicality. The raciologists of Europe's imperial period worked to give Hegel's famous speculations a blunt facticity. The theatre of history was indeed the temperate zone. Recognizing the extent of this pattern, its enduring power, and the legacy of its claims upon academic historiography, geography, and philosophical anthropology is another necessary step toward appreciating how the idea of history as a narrative of racial hierarchy and racial conflict helped to undo modernity's best promises.

A different history, composed of critical reflections on the idea of "race," forms an essential part of the background to what I want to argue below. It has sometimes been judged to be disreputable but nonetheless creates a larger sense of intellectual work than the one that scholastic life provides. Recognizing this history demands the appreciation of interventionist and dissident work by numerous writers who, like the towering figures of W. E. B. DuBois and C. L. R. James, had intermittent, insecure, or ambivalent relations with institutions of higher learning. Bringing greater legitimacy to that tradition of oppositional reflection can deliver us into a novel space where, as part of a survey of the relationship between the modern world and the elaboration of racial categories, we cannot avoid consideration of the relationships between race thinking, historiography, historicality and the sometimes evasive, normative codes of white supremacism.

It should be clear from this declaration that I want to defend what has lately become a rather unfashionable orientation toward manifestations of "race" in the political field. I am disinclined to accept the power of racial divisions as anterior to politics or see them as an inescapable, natural force that conditions consciousness and action in ways that merely political considerations simply cannot match. These refusals help to prepare for the difficult task of making critical, historical, and philosophical encounters with racism productive. This, in turn, requires seeing "race" as moral as well as political and analyzing it as part of a cosmopolitan understanding of the damage that racisms are still doing to democracy.

The Souls of Cosmopolitan Folk

The centenary of DuBois' great book *The Souls of Black Folk* arrived recently. It was celebrated anxiously, amidst great turbulence in geopolitical affairs. The opportunity to reflect upon that landmark publication again and to engage it in relation to our own circumstances seems especially valuable at the moment because it affords a chance to consider the distinctive *worldliness* of DuBois' humanist thinking, which has something to offer our own predicament in the midst of globalization and the planetary consequences of resurgent U.S. imperial power. DuBois' book was underpinned by a cosmopolitan imagination, which, in turn, shaped the way that he was able to make his experiences of displacement and relocation—inside as well as outside the U.S. national state—useful and appealing to readers who were remote from his immediate circumstances. I have made a detailed commentary on the book elsewhere. However, I want to return to a few of the problems that it raises again now in order to draw out DuBois' clever balancing of local and global considerations. His skill in that delicate operation can still teach us something in a different century where the color line cannot be the problem that it was in the past and the relationship between the particular and the universal is being constantly reconsidered in the light of several important developments for which the term "globalization" supplies a rather inadequate shorthand. Our scope for action is bounded, on the one hand, by the advent of a translocal human-rights culture that has resonated in every corner of the planet. On the other hand, we confront the need to defend the international institutional order that was composed in the debris that DuBois would describe in 1947 as "the collapse of Europe."[2] This must be done in order to prevent the recurrence of conflict and to consolidate governmental and judicial schemes above the level of national states.

Those processes are connected to the elaboration of economic, medical, and environmental problems that are beyond the control of national governments, to the technological and cultural revolution that has changed the relationship between information and power, to the collapse of official communism, and to the worldwide shift in gendered and generational relations that has expanded conceptions of citizenship and altered all settlements between women and men, parents and children, even the great majority who live within the realm of scarcity. This brief inventory endorses a view of the historical and economic machinery of globalization that has become orthodox. It needs to be amended because it has failed to appreciate the impact of decolonization, which provides another neglected strand in the unfolding of political antagonisms on a global scale.

In trying to grasp the specificity of this situation, we are often tempted, just as DuBois was before us, to reach for the ideas of world history and world citizenship. These notions were imported into his political thought from their obvious German sources. Many contemporary commentators regard these " metanarratives" as deeply problematic, but his stubborn commitment to them provided more or less constant margins for his shifting political outlook even when his strategic affiliations shifted and his tactical commitments wavered and evolved. Those attachments were articulated in different ways with his socialism and his pan-Africanism. Indeed, his intimate relationship with these fundamental ideas extended far beyond the simple, reformist goals of securing the admission of Africa into world history and of the Negro into world citizenship.

The essays brought together in *The Souls of Black Folk* presented DuBois' first, but in many ways his most compelling attempts to reconcile the contending attractions of people, race, and nation and to harness them into a higher service that can be defined as the figuration of a modern humanity shorn of its historic attachments to racism and equipped with a renewed concept of raceless democracy to match its aspirations toward social progress as well as its progressive political agenda. DuBois' repeated specification of the twentieth century as the century of the color line makes vivid sense in the setting provided by his progressive impulses. Rather than arguing that we were forever to be trapped in racism's hall of mirrors, he was elevating Jim Crow to a problem of world-historic proportions. He drew powerfully on a Hegelian conceptual architecture in which, for example, the coupled strivings of those warring ideals, that famous American Negro "twoness," would eventually be sublated into a "better truer self." Thus, for him, Negro folk song was not only "the sole American music," it was also a "beautiful expression of *human* experience" (emphasis added). Once the nineteenth century had been understood as "the first century of human sympathy," he could discover and promote the novel patterns of reciprocal human recognition that would create vital alternatives to the terminally alienated relations in which races encountered one another in a radically alienated manner as human and infrahuman. This would move society past the blockage where liberty, justice, and right were marked "For White People Only."

Thinking again about his well-known formulations today, I want to suggest that DuBois was either ambivalent or a little disingenuous about whether the limits of African American political struggle could be adequately defined through the goal of making "it possible for a man to be both a Negro and an American" without being abused, and indeed about whether the rather modest result involved in becoming "a co-worker in the kingdom of culture" was, in his view, really sufficient to redress the residual wrongs of recently ended racial slavery. The issue of his worldliness returns with these questions.

Those overly modest aims mask the broader political and philosophical dimensions of an argument that was certainly directed toward the unreceptive national state and its Jim Crow government but also aimed beyond those authorities to another constituency. He calls this object "The World." His portentous conclusion to *Souls* says that the wilderness into which he immodestly feared his vibrant book might fall was "the world wilderness" and argues poetically that the problem with racial hierarchy was that it made "a mockery" and "a snare" of human brotherhood. These observations did not prevent him from upholding rather than rejecting what is today the unfashionable possibility that human brotherhood might be rescued from those temporary conditions. After all, "Negro blood" had a message for the wider world beyond the narrow American space where the various disabilities intrinsic to the country's traditional racial order had unexpectedly gifted blacks with second sight and, through their sublime sufferings, furnished humanity as a whole with conceptions of freedom and democracy more elaborate and profound than anything previously known.

As one might anticipate, DuBois links disability and victimage with the possibility of acquiring richer varieties of consciousness. Their appearance in North America, Hegel's land of the future, was also important to him. The connection between liberation from racial hierarchies and the future, the yet to come, allowed DuBois to dream forward and thus to remake the map of world civilizations in the interest of what we can call the worldly, or even the cosmopolitan Negro. But that was not the end of his argument, which is rather more complex than some of its recent canonical reconfigurations have allowed it to be. The world becomes a different place once the history of black resistance in the Western Hemisphere has been added to our understanding of it, and an acknowledgement of the protracted suffering of African-descended peoples outside of Africa has contributed to the overdue redefinition of its fluctuating moral conscience. DuBois' Hegelian scheme allows this to be done not in the narrow interest of world history's victims but, provocatively, in the contested name of humanity in general. Its advocates are marginal folk whose brutal history and traumatic experience are not usually foregrounded by this variety of universal rhetoric.

The reduction of human brotherhood to a mockery was achieved by the exclusionary force of racism. The snare DuBois speaks of seems to lie in underestimating how much has to be done in order to repair and rework facile notions of human fellowship and solidarity, whether they are religious or liberal. To imagine that these are easy or straightforward tasks is a major error that can be avoided only if the corrosive power of the broken world's racial order can be addressed seriously and consistently. This racial order or nomos cannot be undone by fiat, by charity, or by goodwill and must enter comprehensively into the terms of political culture. It is only then, in the face of a whole, complex, planetary history of suffering, that the luxury and the risk of casual talk about humanity can be sanctioned.

To make better sense and use of this difficult stance today, we need to see where the local tradition of insight in which DuBois' work stands began to resonate with global problems—for example, where it became connected with the terror and bitterness of imperial war and gradual decolonization and where it spoke to the disenchanted acquisition of what are now called human rights by peoples who had only recently been accepted by their colonizers and racial betters as human beings. We should also recall that when the African American savant wrote those celebrated words, he had yet to see the catastrophe of the First World War, never mind the Second. The words "Auschwitz," "Hiroshima," "gulag," and "Apartheid" were unknown to him, and the idea of genocide did not form part of the conceptual apparatus through which he considered the moral credentials of North America's color-coded modernity and the ethical pretensions of western civilization.

We are, unlike DuBois, now obliged to note that white supremacy is only one among a variety of depressing options in the unwholesome cornucopia of absolutist thinking about "race" and ethnicity. The resolute enthusiasm of postmodern ethnic cleansers and absolutists apparently knows no color lines. Hendrik Verwoerd, Samuel Huntington, Ariel Sharon, Slobodan Milosevic, Osama bin Laden, Condoleeza Rice, and a host of others have all contributed something to the belief that absolute culture rather than color is more likely to supply the organizing principle that underpins contemporary schemes of racial classification and division. These distinctions may be far removed from warring totalities of blackness and whiteness but are nonetheless likely to be scarred by the Manichaean relationship they exemplify.

The waning of the raciological markers associated with high imperialism has proved no obstacle to the multiplication of hostility and hatred. On the contrary, the desire to purify groups and homogenize communities—especially if they are to be readied to withstand the trials of globalization and unchallenged U.S. imperial power—seems to have become more intense. This is true especially where lines of demarcation formerly produced by racial or ethnic markers have been blurred by intermarriage and other, anxiety-inducing intimacies that underline the absurdity and triviality of ever racializing difference.

Race thinking has proliferated, but in order to maintain its grip on the world, it has had to change. The simpler *hatreds* forged in more innocent days now coexist with complex, proteophobic, and ambivalent patterns.[3] This change means that blackness can sometimes connote prestige rather than the unadorned inferiority of "bare life" on the lowest rungs of humanity's ontological ladder. Under these conditions, the boundaries between contending groups must repeatedly be made anew and may only be respected when they have been marked out in warm blood.

These developments, which DuBois and his peers could not have anticipated, mean that we must also be prepared to amend the interpretative agenda he set more than a hundred years ago for what would eventually become anti-racist humanism, rooted in and articulated with the democratic aspirations of twentieth-century socialism and Feminism.

Barely a decade after his famous words about the color line, DuBois had been able to turn his gaze outward, away from the United States and toward the significance of racial divisions for the dynamic of progress in the modern world. He summoned the planet's radical intelligentsia to First Universal Races Congress in London with these words in the pages of *The Crisis* magazine:

> The congress is the meeting of the World on a broad plane of human respect and equality. In no other way is human understanding and world peace and progress possible. . . . Only then in a world-wide

contact of men in which the voices of all races are heard shall we begin that contact and sympathy which in God's time will bring out of war and hatred and prejudice a real democracy of races and nations. . . . To such a meeting should go particularly those people to whom the physical differences of race and nation are ridiculous or incomprehensible . . . and those who cannot see that the canons of morality extend beyond their own family or nation, or color of skin. From such a congress should come the beginnings of vast tolerance and sympathy. Not only a tolerance of the Chinese and Hindus on the part of Europeans, but just as necessary comprehension of European thought and morality on the part of millions of darker peoples, who have slight cause to view it with respect. We may sympathize with world-wide efforts for moral reform and social uplift, but before them all we must place those efforts which aim to make humanity not the attribute of the arrogant and the exclusive, but the heritage of all men in the world where most men are colored."[4]

These sentences provide a reminder that though the critical orientation toward our relation with our racial selves is an evasive thing, often easier to feel than to express, it does have important historical precedents. Even in its cruder forms, this cosmopolitan mentality prompts exciting questions, some of which were foreshadowed in DuBois's own development: Can race-hierarchy that has been built on residual eighteenth-century classifications survive? Will it be able to structure the political cultures of the twenty-first century in ways that are similar to the power it enjoyed in the eras of colonial empires, European imperial statecraft, and Cold War geopolitics? After that "color line," then what? What are raciological differences becoming next, in a world where our understanding of humanity has been irrevocably reshaped by genomics, biotechnologies and self-conscious biocolonialism? Is race politics a nontransferable North American accomplishment? What does it contribute to the diverse processes that are shaping very different multicultural environments and polities in Europe, South Africa, Australia, Canada, and Palestine, all conditions far from the casual segregation that formed DuBois in Great Barrington, Massachusetts? We should not be tempted into a reading of his ancient invocation of the color line as a suggestion that "race" is a fatal, unchanging principle of political cultures that stretches unbroken and infinite into a future that is defined, just as the past was, precisely by the violent force of racial divisions. My refusal of that fate is what defines the approach to anti-racist agency I want to sketch out.

Races and Cultures

As I understand it, the project DuBois initiated does not only look toward cosmopolitan culture for a transcendental antidote to the damage produced by "race." Instead, it invites us to lament the failures of parochial culture and local politics where they are defeated by mistaken and parochial attachments to "race." Those lapses are most likely to occur when "race" is reified as embodiment or represented as a mysterious and self-evident force, unrelated to history and immune to the effects of conscious action. This is probably a good opportunity to emphasize that by "race" I do not mean physical variations or differences commonsensically coded in, on, or around the body. For me, "race" refers primarily to an impersonal, discursive arrangement, the brutal result of the raciological ordering of the world, not its cause. Tracking the term directs attention toward the manifold structures of a racial nomos—a legal, governmental, and spatial order—that, as we have seen, is now reviving the geopolitical habits of the old imperial system in discomforting ways. I hope that this line of inquiry can raise important historical and conceptual problems about the distinctiveness and continuities of colonial power and government, especially where it has been armored in ignorance and fortified by color-coded disdain. In the long term, this stance turns our thinking toward Apartheid and the other related political technologies for managing segregated populations that are common to diverse colonial histories.

The proposed stance draws upon the insight displayed by the brave mid-twentieth century thinkers who built upon DuBois' approach. In their work—both practical and theoretical—we can find a political imagination that is equal to the breadth of his original call to the conference-going world elite. Characteristically, the work of these thinkers braids a number of themes. Their confrontations with Nazism were tied to the possibility of armed anticolonial resistance and to some powerful commitments to civil- and human-rights struggles. These events and themes combined to produce a philosophically grounded analysis of racism and its political dimensions in several different places, not all of which are obviously or immediately colonial in character.

Even a cursory genealogy of these positions would have to combine the voices of DuBois, James, Senghor, and the rest with insights drawn from the writings of European commentators like Eric Voegelin, Emmanuel Levinas, and Hannah Arendt, all of whom stumbled into the same political and moral terrain and deployed the resources of their great scholarship to confront the potency of race thinking, in many cases struggling with the unsettling implications of their unlooked-for discoveries.

Tracing the unfolding of the new world tradition that DuBois inaugurated even further into the twentieth century, it becomes important to focus upon the way that the distinction between human and civil rights has functioned in black political thought. Consider Malcolm X's vivid account of his own transoceanic epiphany:

> Both ways on a plane across the Atlantic I was studying a document about how the United Nations proposes to insure the human rights of the oppressed minorities of the world. The American black man is the world's most shameful case of minority oppression. What makes the black man think of himself as only an internal United States issue is just a catch-phrase, two words "civil rights." How is the black man going to get "civil rights" before he wins his *human* rights? If the American black man will start thinking about his *human* rights, and then start thinking of himself as one of the world's great peoples, he will see he has a case for the United Nations.[5]

The worthwhile twentieth-century project to which these words give testimony spanned the overdeveloped and developing worlds. For brevity's sake, its contemporary successor might now be conceptualized as a deliberate development of the translocal interpretations of "race," racism, culture, belonging, and identity that were first laid out in the complex and forbidding "new humanism" of Frantz Fanon, where black political thought was challenged to advance an interpretation of past and present sufferings with reference to the future.[6] Pursuit of a partisan history of the postcolonial present that can inform anti-racist practice could do far worse than be guided by the irreverent spirit evident in Fanon's youthful flirtations with an existentialist understanding of human agency as well as his appetite for a "new humanism" that could, for example, give the human element in human rights a more worthwhile content than the default settings specified by either Cold War liberalism or its more recent, heavily armored varieties.

The willingness to imagine or invent political cultures capable of ending racism now demands a variety of creative work similar to Fanon's own. Of course, that decisive "refusal to accept the present as definitive" is not as easy as he made it sound fifty years ago when the failures of western European civilization were apparent to everyone and the destructive capacity of race thinking was impossible to ignore.

The youthful Fanon trumpeted his decisionistic escape from the constraints of inherited circumstance in the closing sections of *Black Skin, White Masks*, but he was operating in a framework of analysis informed by substantial elements of historical materialism. That affiliation was articulated together with the distinctive "constructionist" problematic that flowed from his intimacies with the work of Sartre and Beauvoir. This combination grows in importance when we grasp its refusals of scholastic protocol. Fanon used it to strip not only the Negro but also the idea of "race" itself of the ontological claims that removed them from history and delivered them instead to the unnatural realm of what he called "timeless truths" and "ultimate radiances." This radical approach refers us back to the race-making processes he had identified in the opening pages of the same work as "sociogeny," a rather valuable and oddly neglected concept. His attachment to what Sylvia Wynter has called "the sociogenetic principle" encompasses but also moves beyond a radical historicising of racism that requires alertness to its changing forms and functions.

For Fanon, the ontology of races becomes historical and the universal, and the particular can enter into a new relationship from which the possibility of novel forms of humanity can derive:

> Is it not obvious that there can only be a white race? What would "white people" correspond to? . . . The truth is that there is nothing, a priori to warrant the assumption that any such thing as a Negro People exists. That there is an African people, that there is a West Indian people, this I do believe. But when someone talks to me about that "Negro people," I try to understand what is meant. Then, unfortunately, I understand that there is in this a source of conflicts. Then I try to destroy this source.[7]

Fanon allowed for the possibility that "time lags" and "differences of rhythm" could arise in the systematic flow of racialized mentalities and identifications. He saw too that the symbolic constructs, imaginary representations, and political meanings that derived from discrete phases in the history of "races" could coexist, interact, and combine. The biopolitical force of the colonial order was, for example, supplemented but never completely erased by the culturalist, anthropologically minded race thinking of the 1950s. It was then, in the bloody penumbra of the Third Reich, that innocent culture took over from raw natural hierarchy as the favored medium through which racial differences would become apparent as common sense.

The emergence of genomic theories of "race" has left those constructions in a residual condition. However, like abandoned munitions under an old battlefield, though they may be obsolete, they are nonetheless powerful. Indeed, the passage of time may have added to their volatility even as the rigid racial hierarchy they once created has lost many of its attractions.

Simple, mechanical conceptions of racial difference now offer no plausible therapy capable of salving the visceral anxieties and pre-political concerns that speak to the currency of "race" and absolute ethnicity not only in the lives of subordinate groups—gilding their traditional badges of inferiority—but in the increasing fears of those who feel themselves to be superior but find that the postcolonial world withholds automatic assent to their historic demand for power and recognition.

Pursuing the conflict between those groups further into the world of colonial rule, Fanon presents the Manichaean opposition of those huge, color-coded aggregates "black" and "white" as a catastrophe. Wherever this arrangement has been established, patterns of intermixture and cosmopolitan combination were erased. In a profound change that represents the inauguration of the race-friendly, colonial order, intercultural relations that were more complex and more fluid were replaced by this simpler, bipolar antagonism. All of that event's original violence was then concentrated in a condensed and suspended but nonetheless traumatic form, inside the language of racial imperatives. Repudiation of those dualistic pairings—black/white, settler/native, colonizer/colonized—has become an urgent political and moral task. Like the related work of repairing the damage they have so evidently done, it can be accomplished via a concept of *relation*. This idea refers historians and critics of racism to the complex, tangled, profane and sometimes inconvenient forms of interdependency. It supplies a productive starting point for the work Fanon described as "dis-alienation," by which he meant the unmaking of racialized bodies and their restoration to properly human modes of being in the world.[8]

Before we can deal with the historical conditions that supported these racial identities and, during Europe's imperial preeminence, made them translocal, bringing pure and irreconcilable racial and ethnic entities into being and then baptizing them with blood, we should address the *principles* of solidarity and collectivity that produced "races" as totalities. These novel aggregations were to be governed by distinctive procedures that are inseparable from the political rules and mystified ontological foundations of Europe's national states, their colonial offshoots, and the military and juridical qualifications introduced into their governance by the dictates of imperial rule.

This orientation requires a lengthy detour through the political philosophies of tacitly as well as openly racialized modernity. These forms of knowledge need to be reconsidered in the light of their colonial and imperial provenance. Theories and concepts, notions of history and culture, government and statecraft can be found to have been contingently implicated in the workings of European domination that they subsequently rationalized and legitimated, but that is not the whole story. Without lapsing into an idealist approach to the history of raciological ideas, we can also recognize the modern, ontologically infused discourses of "race" and nation as having had a larger, world-historic significance than most historians of imperial power have so far been willing to grant. The recent demonization of "sand niggers" and "towel heads" testifies to this as much as the sudden appearance of the malevolent alien enemies that today's tacit race thinking is eager to dismiss as "apocalyptic nihilists" whose desire for martyrdom, announced in their illegitimate cry from the global South, can only be answered by the blessed bombs and sanctified bullets of that ultimate colonial fantasy, a clean war.[9]

If the rational irrationalities of raciology are acknowledged as a driving element in the development of both imperial statecraft and modern political theory, this kind of inquiry can be used to dispute conventional conceptions of the relationship between metropolitan state and colonial outpost, between core and periphery. This shift generates a view of the colony as rather more than an extractive commercial operation. No longer merely a settlement, an adventure, an opportunity, a place for self-creation, self-discovery, and a space of death, it can be recognized as a laboratory, a location for experiment and innovation that transformed the exercise of governmental powers at home and configured the institutionalization of imperial knowledge to which the idea of "race" was central.[10]

We must ask not only how the distinctive political and juridical dynamics of colonial power may have been shaped by the articulation of racial discourses and the belief in racial difference but also how the political relations constituted in the core of the old imperial systems would be transformed as a result of murderous enthusiasm for the proper racial ordering of the world. Those ambitions had been conceptualized long before Europe's colonies initiated a secondary diaspora by exporting living labor as well as commodities and raw materials. Rather than simply representing the novel calculus of an indifferent economic rationality, these developments manifested the impact of a moral and political economy that placed a discrete value on the subordination, confinement, and destruction of racialized bodies. This outlook is condensed into Sir Garnett Wolesley's sage vision of the civilizing mission of colonial domination:

> The more one associates with the African Negro, the stronger becomes the impression that he is no more suited to stand alone than a white child would be. Until he learns to do voluntarily his share of daily work in this great domain which God has ordered

man to till and cultivate, it is in my opinion better for the Negro and for the world that he should learn discipline under an enlightened but very strict master.[11]

Colonial Politics

This revised view of the place of race in political culture necessitates further adjustments to the way that politics has been understood. As far as orthodox histories of European statecraft are concerned, problems like the disappearance of public torture are often understood to identify a significant stage in the development of a new type of power: capillary, biopolitical, and primarily directed toward the management of population. Against this assumption, the history of colonial power overflows with evidence that suggests that a distinctive association of governance with military power and martial law should be identified and that this association with distinctive forms of governmental calculation changed the workings of institutional complexes like the army and medical practice, as well as the professional thinking of colonial administrators, planners, and managers.[12] There were different biopowers at work in these colonial histories, and they did not remain sealed off from the mainstream at the distant ends of the imperial system.[13]

Focusing on the colonial mutation of basic institutional components of state power—sovereignty, territory, population, and government itself—raises numerous issues that complicate and can even overturn conventional accounts of how modern political authority was secured and then changed by its imperial missions and the ideas about "race" that made them possible. This worthwhile corrective exercise yields more than an amended account of biopolitical government, which is seen differently when it is approached from imperial angles.[14] A fuller appreciation of specifically colonial input into modern statecraft promises an altogether different sense of where bio-political procedures and anthropological hierarchies might fit into an amended history of modernity, understood now as what Enrique Dussel calls "trans-modernity," a geopolitical project with a longer reach and more profound consequences than is customarily appreciated.[15]

The significance of this conceptual adjustment can only increase if the resulting colonial modernity or transmodernity can be shown to have relied upon investments in the idea of racial hierarchy both at home and abroad. Most commentators on these dynamic threads of planetary history have failed to mention "race" specifically or to entertain the possibility that histories of racism and raciology might be productively associated with the lineages of political anatomy and biopower that culminated in the ideal of the Apartheid state and the paradigmatic forms of spatial separation—in dwelling and in transit—with which it is still associated. This connection is not only evident in the obvious cases like Israel's heavily fortified dominion over occupied Palestinian territories but in the more general mechanisms of what Andre Gorz called the "south africanisation" of social life in the overdeveloped world. Gorz's useful term derives from his reading of the "pre-revolutionary" phase of South African political culture, but I think it travels well and can still illuminate the export of many social and economic relations associated historically with colonial societies into the heartlands and hubs of overdevelopment. The appeal of security and the related appearance of gated and secured residential spaces are two important components of this larger change. The proliferation of service work and the reappearance of a caste of servile, insecure, and underpaid domestic laborers, carers, cleaners, deliverers, messengers, attendants, and guards are surely others. The segmentation and casualization of employment, health, and dwelling are the foundations on which these aspects of the privatization and destruction of the civic order have come to rest.

For political theory, the desacralization of the body rightly became another major issue in accounting for the transition toward modern authority as well as understanding the development of historical and institutional conditions in which it becomes possible to treat people as refuse.[16] Tracking that important theme through the space of colonial government provides me with a means to explore a number of analytical possibilities. They emerge with the change of focus that makes racism a substantive theoretical and political problem in the history of transmodern government. The role of race thinking in rendering the bodies of natives, slaves, and other infrahumans worthless or expendable is a pivotal issue in specifying how the racialization of governmental practice impacted upon the pragmatic exercise of colonial power.[17] The vengeful aftermath of the Indian uprising of 1857 has always been discussed as an example of the British civilizing mission in action. Legal procedures were set aside in circumstances where the military officers who became judge, jury, and executioner could not understand the languages of those they put to death. Sir John Kaye's massive *History of the Sepoy War in India* describes the carnival of death which met the rebels in colorful terms. In one area they were killed "amidst every possible indignity that could be put upon them by our soldiers under the approving smiles of their officers." In another, "military officers were hunting down criminals of all kinds, and hanging them with as little compunction as though they had been pariah dogs or jackals, or vermin of a baser kind." He continues, "one gentleman boasted of the number he had finished off 'in quite an artistic manner,' with mango-trees for gibbets and elephants for drops, the victims of this wild justice being strung up as though for pastime, in the form of a figure of eight." Alongside the aesthetic aspects of this scene, its "wildness" and its apparently playful character communicate the colonial order's peculiar mix of terror with law. Karl Marx, writing in the *New-York Daily Tribune* shortly after the event, drew attention to the place of racism in this bloody ritual by quoting one enthusiastic participant who reported "We hold court-martials on horseback, and every nigger we meet we either string up or shoot."

In the historiography of 1857, the practice of blasting prisoners to death by tying their bodies over the mouths of cannon has proved controversial, particularly among those commentators who strive to keep the administration of the Empire unsullied by cruelty. One recent revisionist historian of this episode has provided an interesting example of the melancholic results involved in avoiding condemnation of this practice by insisting that it should be seen in context. He argues firstly, that this technique was introduced into India by the Moguls rather than the British and so they should not to be blamed unreasonably for adopting it, secondly, that it was an honorable death, and, thirdly, that it was employed as an act of deterrence rather than of vengeance. In a peculiar act of retrospective pseudo-sympathy with the victims, this mode of killing gets represented as, in effect, a humane option to be judged morally only by the rapidity with which death arrived. The vastly more interesting issue of what this grisly spectacle might have meant and done to its British organizers, spectators, and enthusiasts gets smuggled out of sight. One contemporary observer found these hi-tech executions to be "a most sickening sight." Her account has the additional virtue of insisting that the experience of onlookers who were covered by blood and fragments of flesh should be taken into account, to say nothing of the plight of an unfortunate bystander who was hit by one of the vanished prisoners' flying heads that, singed but intact, fell back to earth from a height of several hundred feet.[18]

If the circumstances of this particular orgy of imperial brutality seem too mired in a national liberation struggle or relate too closely to what some revisionist historians represent as a contentious case in which gross violence was evident on both sides, a host of comparable and equally revolting examples can be drawn from diverse places and phases of colonial rule. In Australia and the United States, the history of dealings between governments and the indigenous occupants of their territories is also replete with evidence of a total warfare that fully substantiates James Gump's description of it as "imperial overrule." Two brief illustrations, one from each location, will suffice here.

George Arthur, lieutenant governor of Van Diemen's Land, was one colonial administrator who was drawn, in spite of his own disinclination to needless bloodshed, into a genocidal pattern. Here too a proclamation of martial law proved critical in bringing about "the destruction" of an indigenous population:

> The customary plan adopted toward them . . . was that of attempting to capture the chiefs of the warrior tribes. The Civil authorities, aided by a few of the military, occasionally guided by one of the sable natives, scoured the bush and when the mobs were fallen in with, it depended on the leaders of a party in what manner the natives were to be treated; occasionally they were all shot, or had their brains knocked out by the butt-end of the muskets—other more merciful leaders captured them and brought them to Hobart Town to await the destination the Executive Council might think proper to award them.[19]

The limited range of options—death, confinement, or deportation— would change very little over time, though the balance between them altered as colonial killing power improved and there was increased temptation to imagine that the natives could be made to simply disappear.

The North American "Indian wars" of the late nineteenth century are very well known though seldom subjected to the comparative historical treatment that they demand. The enormous volume of materials involved rightly inhibits hasty generalization, but it is evident even from a limited range of sources that a "nits make lice" approach was repeatedly apparent in the context of these conflicts: "there seemed to be indiscriminate slaughter of men, women and children. There were some thirty or forty squaws collected in a hole for protection; they sent out a little girl about six years old with a white flag on a stick; she had not proceeded but a few steps when she was shot and killed. All the squaws in the hole were afterwards killed . . . [they] offered no resistance."[20]

My central point is that wherever they were applied, the colonial techniques of indiscriminate mass destruction ended up being closer to the work of extermination than control and settlement. In this bloody sequence, the doctrine of preemptive strikes and the systematic refusal to distinguish combatants from civilians have acquired an elaborate and multinational prehistory. From another distant corner of the globe, Roger Casement's 1903 report of his fact-finding journey on behalf of the British

Foreign Office to the upper Congo overflows with the lurid details of governmental terror creatively and legally applied as a mode of political administration and economic exploitation. These words of his, which preface a collection of native testimony about the terrible violence of the period, supply important clues as to what the Belgian King Léopold II's hopes for his colony had become at ground level: "In most of the fights then the natives were merely trying to defend themselves and their homes from attacks made by black soldiers sent to punish them for some failure to do their duty to the State: and if the cause for war was weak, the way in which it was carried out was often revolting."[21]

The countless tales of colonial brutality are too important to be lightly or prematurely disposed of. They cannot capture the whole complexity of imperial affairs, but these days they tend to get overlooked because a sanitized history of the imperial project is required by those who wish to bring it back to life. My argument is that these accounts of colonial war must be owned so that they can become useful in understanding the empire, in making sense of its bequest to the future and its impact on the moral and political contents of British national identity, and perhaps also in the task of understanding what racism contributes to the distinctive tempo of colonial politics and government.

Info-war images of the shackled, goggled, humbled, and orange-suited "battlefield detainees" incarcerated at the U.S. government's Cuban "Camp Delta" suggest that an economy of colonial alterity may still be operative, conditioning the operations of law and governmental power in exceptional places and emergency times. Though he is uninterested in either racial discourse or in the analysis of colonial relations, there is something profound to learn from Giorgio Agamben's attempts to reconcile the theoretical insights of Arendt and Foucault in this area.[22] He has made a dense but invigorating study of sovereign power that is centered on the politically ambivalent and juridically marginal figure of the person who can be killed with impunity and of their reduction to the infrahuman condition of "bare life" that sanctions their death. The problem he describes is not just present in disputes over habeas corpus or primarily a matter of concern for isolated and exceptionally vulnerable individuals whose undervalued bodies have also been endowed with the redeeming fiction of legal personality.

Like the technique of preemptive attack, the space of wild justice suggests that those comforting projections were never accepted by colonial powers. Histories of conquest and famine alike reveal that colonial government contributed to the manifestation of bare life in historically unprecedented quantities and circumstances under the supervision of administrative and managerial systems that operated by the rules of raci-ology and qualified the dictates of ruthless economic logic accordingly.[23] It is not just that rationally applied terror routinely became imperial administration but also that the critical figure of the person who could be killed with impunity or disposed of without conscience moved out of the liminal position to which it had been allocated by the unruffled workings of the national state. That vulnerable figure could merge easily with those of the infrahuman native and the racial slave, the negro, the aboriginal and the indigene. At that fateful point, the colonial project not only man-ifested a new kind of geopolitical space but filled it with a new cast of readily racialized characters.[24]

The lowly life forms that populate the militarized quarter and exist under the pressure of emergency powers exhibit the full shocking insub-stantiality of their infrahuman character only when their bare lives are contrasted with the healthier modes of being enjoyed by the invading armies or the settler population and its distant relatives in the mother country. These different types were products of a colonial enterprise that mandated the reduction of the native to a status below that of an animal in order to operate properly. The insubordinate native, always closer to both death and scarcity, stood at the epicenter of governmental action, placed there by the imperatives of exploitation and kept there by pro-gressively more elaborate racial anthropologies that, however potent they appeared to be, could never, according to Fanon anyway, completely "mask the human realities" involved. He, of course, wrote long before the routinization of government by spin and censorship and the consolidation of the culture of indifference associated with consumerism and imperial overdevelopment.

From these perspectives, the colony can once again be identified as a special kind of place. Its necessary reliance on divisions *within* humankind, for example, demanded and institutionalized the abolition of all concep-tions of citizenship as universal entitlement. This particular change might also be used to represent the end or limit of politics as it had been previ-ously understood. The passbook and the identification card were the inno-vations that characterized the new order. A new set of geopolitical habits emerged here too. Propaganda became more prominent, and distinctive killing technologies appropriate to testing encounters with infrahumanity could be refined.[25]

Though they have had little scholastic currency until recently, the dis-puted significance of these connections between colonial and metropolitan life was central to the political and moral agenda devised by the national liberation movements of the twentieth century. Their core questions included asking whether the Nazi genocide had colonial precedents, whether the West's continuing colonial empires reproduced or converged with the raciology that had lent its logic to the Third Reich's crimes, whether Europe could recover, and whether capitalism could be divested of its historic attachments to racial division. This provocative inventory is still unresolved.

In crossing this ground, Fanon describes the process through which colonial subjects are rendered vulnerable to the forms of rationality, violence, and legality that can be routinely visited upon the paradoxical conditions of social death and exclusionary inclusion that Agamben identifies with the concept of bare life. Fanon suggests that this result is not an aberration but a routine arrangement associated with both the pragmatic and the theoretical functioning of colonial authority and power. It is significant also that he contrasts the practical morality, which guides native resistance against the resulting pressure downward, with the overly abstract forms of the wholesome universalism that is more likely be found at the other end of the imperial chain.[26]

A proper appreciation of this difference in ethical outlooks can be deduced from understanding the natives' pursuit of a concrete and immediate dignity in response to their suffering. That reaction is their first answer to the dehumanization involved in the institution of race hierarchy. Humanity can only be recovered by would-be postcolonial subjects, Fanon continues, through a new relation to the land that "will bring . . . bread and, above all, dignity." Territory thus supplies an "essential value" in the economy of colonial reparations that inevitably also includes the counterviolence and resentment of the natives, the slaves, and the unfree.

This geopolitical and spatial aspect of power is intrinsic to Fanon's analysis of the colonial order of "race," its nomos. I want to emphasize that for him the spatial configuration of brutal colonial government was *not* a question of politics. The political as Europe knew it simply did not exist there. Instead, the emergence of race-coded duality marked the suspension of political relations and fostered their replacement by a rather different set of what we could call parapolitical technologies and procedures. This innovation helped to make a special brutality—supposedly anachronistic by mid-twentieth-century European standards—into the engine of imperial projects so chronically absurd and yet so total in their infiltration of everyday life that they dared to try and parcel up the earth itself along racial lines. This was done, needless to say, in ways that posed difficult questions to movements that looked only to economic progress as the means to deliver a just and raceless world. It also confounded the insubstantial liberal traditions that have proved incapable of generating what Stan Cohen has called a "sociology of denial."[27]

To recapitulate, then, the ruthless binary logic of colonial government placed black and white, settler and native in mutually antagonistic relation. They were separated spatially, but conceptually their common racialization ensured that they were bound to each other so tightly that each was unthinkable without the proximity and hostility of the other. This distinctive geometry of colonial power is notable for the stress it placed on recognition and interdependency and the way it pushed cultural questions to the fore: each racial or ethnic type turns out to have its own space where it is at home and can be itself. We should pause over this ecological arrangement to identify some of its other important consequences. One of them can be highlighted through another acknowledgement of Carl Schmitt's deeply problematic theory of politics as the practical and institutional expression of elemental distinctions between friend and enemy.

Karl Löwith, Schmitt's most acute contemporary critic, drew attention to the way that he had advocated "racial identity as the foundation of [the] shared existence" that preceded the drawing of that fateful political line.[28] Schmitt's influential approach can also be interpreted as an attempt to incorporate a Manichaean code into a universal theory of politics and thus to rewrite the tradition of modern political reflection according to the ultranationalist and race-friendly rules which make all political relations conform to the deadly exigencies of imperial foreign affairs. Fanon shared something of Schmitt's geopolitical and philosophical interests in the living room that imperial power awarded to the settler and denied to the native. He saw racial hierarchy as among the first and most durable products of territorial expropriation. The coupling and separation of black and white, settler and native, was central to his account of the governmental arrangements that characterized colonial rule and produced two great camps—totalities that could synthesize unity and plurality into the distinctive patterns associated with the lives of "races." Taking his cue from Freud, Fanon argued that those great racialized "encampments" were permeated with neurosis and a "dual narcissism." The elemental opposition between them refers us back to the primal problem of "minor difference," if not to the essential features of monotheistic systems and their genocidal offshoots. This, perversely, was also his route to a hesitant universality and, perhaps eventually, to the evasive new humanism that he wrote so fondly, so urgently, and so inspirationally about.

The emphasis that Fanon placed upon Manichaeism shows how the relationship between black and white, settler and native, colonizer and colonized, denies any possibility of a comforting dialectical resolution. The omnipresent violence of colonial administration creates the colony as a frozen, immobile world of statues that is not in teleological or progressive motion toward freer, healthier, or more comfortable arrangements. The split character of that militarized colonial world allowed it to be inhabited, in effect, by different species, each of which nourished itself inadequately with the fantasy of its unanimity. Fanon underlines that the breakup of this colonial world "does not mean that . . . lines of communication will be established between the two zones. The destruction of the colonial world is no more and no less than the abolition of one zone, its burial in the depths of the earth or expulsion from the country."

Happily, that bleak scene was not the end of Fanon's colonial tale. Though it is overlooked by many of his more recent interpreters, the status of black and white, settler and native, as political values and ethnic cues recurs finally in his critique of bourgeois nationalism and unsettling account of the postrevolutionary transition. By this time, the original Manichaeism of the settlers, which, as we have seen, culminated in the transformation of the native into either an animal or the quintessence of evil, has been smashed. However, considerable damage is still being done where an inverted but essentially similar adaptation of the settlers' racialized mentality has taken root in the opposite encampment: among the resentful and angry natives.

In Fanon's optimistic scheme, this second, transitional formation yields eventually to a wider consciousness that can break with the alienated logic of epidermalization and open up oppositional, and for the first time fully human consciousness to a wider range of ethical and political sensibilities. This outcome, which, as I have said, is not the third term in a dialectical movement, is also spattered with blood. It provides a reminder that the association of blackness and whiteness is not just a site of ontological obstacles to the emergence of disalienated human consciousness among the oppressed and victimized (which was Fanon's primary concern). He also recognizes that dominance can carry its own wounds, even if they are veiled in colonial privilege and postcolonial melancholia. He is instructive in viewing this racial wound as an amputation. In his scheme, the colonizers' abstract whiteness is never a parallel or complementary "white" version of the culture, history, and consciousness that previously produced the natives' abject "blackness" as an object of anthropological knowledge, colonial exploitation, and racialized power.

The revolutionary stage that marks the end of "race" may also prove to be the starting point for a new form of class analysis prompted by post- and neocolonial varieties of exploitation and authority. This insight arises amidst his consideration of a moment of danger in which the national liberation project can be hijacked and people moving out of alienation are offered back the spurious comforts of racial and ethnic differences in exchange for their human freedom. This disturbing point is clear even from Constance Farrington's translation:

> The people must be taught to cry "stop thief!" . . . the people must give up their too-simple conception of their overlords. The species is breaking under before their very eyes. . . . The barriers of blood and race-prejudice are broken down on both sides. In the same way, not every Negro or Moslem is issued with a hall-mark of genuineness; and the gun or the knife is not inevitably reached for when a settler makes his appearance. Consciousness slowly dawns upon truths that are only partial, limited and unstable. As we may surmise, all this is very difficult.[29]

If we follow Fanon's example and work toward creative possibilities that are too easily dismissed as utopian, our moral and political compass might profitably be reset by acts of imagination and invention that are adequate to the depth of the postcolonial predicament he described. This commitment is part of an approach that has several additional virtues. It can be readily linked to that diminishing and invaluable commodity: hope. And, it can be connected to a vibrant political and ethical enterprise that carries anti-racist dissidence into a deeper confrontation with the history, philosophy, and jurisprudence of "transmodernity."

The innovative emphasis Fanon placed on the social aspect of racial mentalities originally warranted his humanist and existential ventures and marked his departure from the psychologism of his own training. It seems also to have been shaped by the growing conviction that "Marxist analysis should always be slightly stretched every time we have to do with the colonial problem." Today, it still offends attractively against economically deterministic accounts of "race" and racism.

His scurrilous speculations demonstrate the benefits of turning away from the dull priorities established by scholastic reflection on the rational irrationalities of "race" and racism. The limits of that polite labor were reached long ago. Its fruits should certainly be disseminated, but contemporary political strategies must involve more than simply chanting them indefinitely in the optimistic expectation that one day they will be heard by power. The more negative and reflexive orientation I have described draws inspiration from Fanon's determination to make "race" historical and, above all, social. Like him, it assigns racism(s) to the past and can help to make antiracism more than just a jumbled collection of political instruments. It strives to restore a moral credibility to anti-racist critique and to explore the rehabilitation of humanist voices—options that may become more worthwhile today, after the end of natural evolution, than they once were.

Without the crude injustices of racial slavery and colonial conquest to orient us, we are required to know even more comprehensively than in the past precisely what we are against and why. But, as far as the order of racialized differences is concerned, our political imaginations are inclined to falter or become blocked at the point of maximum defensive solidarity. That is where we are certain of what we are against but cannot say what we are *for* with the same degree of clarity and conviction. This hesitancy is associated with several phenomena: Firstly, with the inability to explain how people become intimidated by and resigned to the mystifications of raciality and its narcissism of minor differences; secondly, with how they try to make the refusal to see beyond reified and alienated racial categories into a measure of their political virtue; and lastly, with how—while usually according racial difference a routine and empty measure of recognition as a social and historical construction—they lose the capacity to imagine its unmaking, its deconstruction, its transcendence, or even the possibility of its eventual descent into irrelevance. These problems have sometimes been compounded by a squeamish reluctance to trespass upon the imagined communities of oppressed groups who may have seized the discursive categories through which their subordination has been transacted or imposed and lodged them in the centers of their "wounded" solidarity and the pageant of identities that it supports.

However well-intentioned it may be, the compensatory commitment to absolute unanimity cannot succeed for long. The inevitable appearance of differences within the favored collective creates grave disappointment with any group's lack of spontaneous fellow feeling and mutual regard. Here the ideas of identity, "race," and ethnicity can be seen to have damaged us all over again by feeding expectations of being together that are impossibly high.

The utopian-sounding procedures involved in seeing, thinking, and acting beyond race hierarchy cannot be divorced from practical confrontations with the immediate manifestations of racism. Indeed, I would argue that the ability to imagine political, economic, and social systems in which "race" makes no sense is an essential, though woefully underdeveloped part of formulating a credible antiracism as well as an invaluable transitional exercise. That ability has sadly fallen into disrepute.

These hesitations and inhibitions may be connected to the dominance of anti-humanism in what is left of Left thinking. The pattern of responses

I am criticizing needs to be interpreted as a reaction against the articulation of liberalism and humanism in Cold War discourse as well as a symptom of the scientific pretensions that accompanied the retreat of Marxism and its scholastic turn. Giving antiracism a cosmopolitan history and endowing it with a philosophical skeleton that is not reducible to recent, vaguely Marxist or Feminist commitments helps not only to undermine the growing authority over these matters, which is being invested in dubious figures like Heidegger and Schmitt, but also to answer the apprehensions of those who do not want to accept that it is racism which has made "race" into a burden—on individuals, on polities, and on democracy itself.

Everybody knows that conceptual innovations cannot bring racism to an end, but they do have their uses. They can reveal how sharply scholastic theories diverge from common sense. They can highlight the regrettable fact that the life-threatening jeopardy provoked by being racialized as different is undiminished and may even have increased now that "race" and its certainties can claim to heal or at least calm the anxieties over identity, which have been precipitated by the insecurities and inequalities of globalization.

The academic tribunes of globalization do not usually include the end of formal empires or the wars of decolonization in their accounts of our planet's commercial and political integration. They are mostly a complacent bunch, more content with pondering the enigmas of weightless economic development than the violence that seems to be proliferating around it. This unhealthy situation has redirected attention to the flimsy boundaries placed around racial and ethnic identity by fading national states and desperate political leaders who will try anything to locate the populist pulse of the ailing body politic. The colonial hierarchy that previously specified the proper relation of blackness to whiteness starts to break down. It yields to a different—usually commercial and resolutely antipolitical—understanding of what "races" are and how they differ from themselves and each other. The previously separated worlds of absolutely different groups can then be made to leak. They bleed risk, pleasure, and excitement into one another as part of selling things and accumulating capital. The magic of freshly racialized markets means that it is important to consider whether blackness and whiteness, like raciality's other inventions, should now be understood as nothing but transient symptoms of a dominant but dying order.

It bears repetition that this situation necessitates producing a better history not only of our own planetary movement against racisms but of the political dimensions of racial discourses, which are not peripheral or decorative ideological motifs appended to colonial adventures. They shaped and still embellish the intimate, essential workings of imperial power in ways that confound any oversimple split between material embodiment on the one hand and culture, ideology, and discourse on the other. The history of political struggle that we construct through them does not conform to any neat sociological dichotomy between recognition and redistribution.

At this point, colonial and postcolonial folks can acquire a distinctive mission. Our modern history as disenchanted descendants of people who were themselves commodified for sale on an international market or deemed expendable within the larger racial logic of Europe-centered historical processes, gives us ready access to a fund of knowledge that is useful in a number of areas. These insights are not ours alone but will belong to anybody who is prepared to use them. This history of suffering, rebellion, and dissidence is not our intellectual property, and we are not defenders of cultural and experiential copyright.

Any lessons that can be derived from the histories we have made can furnish resources for the future of this planet. Those lessons do not, of course, aim to redeem past suffering or make it worthwhile. Their very failure to be productive in this way helps to specify that they should be available to anybody who dares, in good faith, to try and set them to work in pursuit of justice. Lastly, it seems imperative to try to revive and sustain those elements of black political culture that are, like DuBois, tolerant, humane, pluralistic, and cosmopolitan in outlook. They are still present in diminishing quantities, but they are muted these days. They have had to take a back seat behind simpler, noisier, and, for many, more attractive options that are in step if not always in tune with the mainstream sentiments of consumer capitalism and have the additional virtue of echoing a seductive nationalist agenda set elsewhere. We cannot be content with the casual proposition that authoritarianism, coercion, and militaristic hierarchy have privileged claims upon that world of blackness and its dissident cultures. We must also ask why our movement has so often been content to build its alternative conceptions of the world from simple inversions of the dismal powers that confront us rather than altogether different conceptions guided by another political morality?

The guiding terms of this Fanonian project—humanism, justice, cosmopolitanism—are all contested. We should doubtless be wary of them because they resonate most strongly with the liberal political thought that has descended from European enlightenment writings. Those attempts to see the lives of individuals and nations in broader contexts supplied by a subversively shifting sense of scale, above all by a sense of the earth as but one small and insignificant location in an infinite and only partially knowable space, are by no means the only forms of cosmopolitan thinking in circulation. The black thinkers of the Western Hemisphere have sometimes been alive to the destiny involved in understanding their own position in planetary terms that confound conventional distinctions between nationalism and cosmopolitanism. The antiracism that inherited a worldly vision from pan-Africanism and passed it on to the anticolonial movements did not descend to the present through the temperate landscape of liberal pieties. It came via disreputable abolitionism and translocal, multicultural, and anti-imperial activism that was allied with the insurrectionary practice of those who, though legally held in bondage, were subject to the larger immoralities of a race-friendly system of domination.

DuBois, James, Fanon, Senghor, and company have already shown that there is a whole counterhistory of modern government to be written from the genealogy of these neglected political formations. They contributed vitality and hope to dissident democratic formations that derived their moral confidence and many of their political dreams from confrontations with the evil and immorality they discovered in the operations of colonial and imperial domination. This opposition confronted and undermined the codes of western liberalism at several significant points. Its principal value is that it can still embarrass and contest the overly innocent versions of liberal thinking that are still in circulation. It highlights their failures in the face of raciology and their refusals to admit the humanity of the racial Other. If we are going to interrupt the romance of racial and ethnic absolutism at last, we will need to find an explanation for how that telling blockage has damaged the planetary movement we should probably no longer refer to minimally and apologetically as antiracism. In recognition of the need for more assertive and wholeheartedly political moods and tactics, we should become prepared to acknowledge the extreme difficulty as well as the great value of moral and political enterprises that require the systematic denaturing of "race" as part of confrontations with the alienated sociality that absorbs the cries of those who suffer by making them sound less than human.

The states of permanent emergency enacted through the declaration of "war against terror" allow minimal scope for active dissent. In many countries dissidence has been criminalized as a minor form of treason, and, where the newly fortified frontier between warring civilizations has been brought to life by info-war and the militarization of everyday life, the desire to presume the equal worth of alien cultures and to offer equal respect in proliferating encounters with otherness is thought to be misguided or out of date. Civilizations are now closed or finished cultures that need to be preserved. The individual agents who are their bearers and affiliates come ready-stamped with iconic badges of relative rank. The languages of "race" and absolute ethnicity ensure that this natural hierarchy, which is also social and cultural, cannot be renegotiated. Today, that ranking increasingly conforms to the dictates of the West's reborn imperial power.

Though it was weakened by networking and the emancipation of capital from many of its local ties, the national state is now being strengthened by the new priority attached to security. Some of the damage done to its institutions by unchecked neoliberal economics has been repaired, and it has emerged once more as the focus of geopolitical conflicts. It is the national state that supplies the cornerstones for any global system of judicial or governmental regulation. The international structures of government and law built up after the defeat of Fascism are no longer as powerful as they were. In the unipolar global order created by the economic and military dominance of the United States, practical geopolitics suggests that the waning authority of bodies like the United Nations is being replaced rather than augmented by a range of new initiatives that derive directly from American strategic objectives, though they are often presented in universalist rhetoric.[1] Even at its most belligerent, this shift has been projected through the benign and seductive language of humanitarianism. On occasions, that idiom has even recast the ideal of imperial power as an "ethical" force which can promote good and stability amidst the flux and chaos of the postcolonial world, where the danger of terrorism by nihilistic nonstate actors and rogue or failing governments looms large. We are told that failed states rather than poverty and hopelessness are the breeding ground of envy and terror.

The meaning and ambition of the term "cosmopolitanism" has been hijacked and diminished by these changes. It still directs our attention toward the relationship between political order and the order found in nature, but the nature in question is now internal to our species and our relationship with ourselves. The discourse of human rights supplies the principal way in which this shared human nature can be made accessible to political debate and legal rationality. This is a rather ethnocentric outcome because the foundational investment that the West has made in the idea of rights is not itself a neutral or universal gesture. Most contemporary debates over human rights, globalization, and justice use "cosmopolitanism" to refer to the elaboration of a supranational system of regulation that opposes or contains the national state from above. The relationship of national states to markets is still contested, but that is insufficient to stop these aggregations from qualifying for recognition as civilizations. In the names of cosmopolitanism and humanitarianism, these particular moral sensibilities can promote and justify intervention in other people's sovereign territory on the grounds that their ailing or incompetent national state has failed to measure up to the levels of good practice that merit recognition as civilized. These adventures, military or economic, may be against the interests of people in the poorer and less developed regions of the earth, but that does not matter. Though they are a majority of people on this planet, they can be overlooked, and their experience is not accepted as part of our world's portrait of itself as a world.

Where their lives and predicament are acknowledged, the armored cosmopolitanism and supposedly benign imperialism that currently promote the cause of improving their lot lack another measure of credibility precisely because they have never paused over the actual history of past imperialism and the ongoing effects of colonial and imperial governance. If the West's innocent commentators were to develop more worldly historical interests, they would discover that previous phases of imperial rule were also regularly described in civilizational and ethical terms. Léopold II, the visionary architect of Belgium's blood-soaked colonial enterprises had, for example, convened the 1876 International Geographical Convention in Brussels with an invitation stressing "the completely charitable, completely scientific and philanthropic nature of the aim to be achieved. It is not a question of a business proposition, it is a matter of a completely spontaneous collaboration between all those who wish to introduce civilization to Africa."[2] Among his noble goals at that time was the suppression of the slave trade in Africa's interior. His opening remarks to that august meeting have become famous as an opportunity to consider the moral worth of European colonial ambitions that would be secured, we should recall, five or six years later by Hiram Maxim's automation and refinement of Victorian civilization's great asset: the machine gun. "The subject which brings us together today is one that deserves in the highest degree to engage the attention of the friends of humanity. To open to civilization the only part of the globe where it has not yet penetrated, to pierce the darkness enshrouding entire populations, that is, if I may venture to say so, a crusade worthy of this century of progress; and I am happy to say how much public sentiment is in favour of its accomplishment. The current is with us."[3]

For any British readers defeated by the sheer volume of our country's imperial historiography or misled into imagining that continentals are more sneaky and immoral than Britain was in the conduct of their imperial administration, Joseph Chamberlain's remarks a few years later at a Royal Colonial Institute dinner in March of 1897 capture the same sort of philanthropic spirit. The have the additional merit of approximating the tone of messianic civilizationism that has been evident in some of the

Blair government's more recent pronouncements about the moral basis of the new imperial order it has been bringing into being. Chamberlain's words must be quoted at length:

> You cannot have omelettes without breaking eggs; you cannot destroy the practices of barbarism, of slavery of superstition, which for centuries have desolated the interior of Africa, without the use of force; but if you will fairly contrast the gain to humanity with the price which we are bound to pay for it, I think you may well rejoice in the result of such expeditions as those which have recently been conducted with such signal success in Nyasaland, Ashanti, Benin, and Nupé—expeditions which may have, and indeed have, cost valuable lives, but as to which we may rest assured for one life lost a hundred will be gained, and the cause of civilization and the prosperity of the people will in the long run be eminently advanced. . . . such a mission as I have described, involves a heavy responsibility. In the wide dominions of the Queen the doors of the temple of Janus are never closed, and it is a gigantic task that we have undertaken when we have determined to wield the sceptre of empire. Great is the task, great is the responsibility, but great is the honour; and I am convinced that the conscience and the spirit of the country will rise to the height of its obligations, and that we shall have the strength to fulfill the mission which our history and our national character have imposed upon us.[4]

Blair's moralism is more usually associated with Gladstone, but his imperialist poses suggest a view of Britain's new liberal and cosmopolitan mission in the world, a view animated by some of the same certainties that guided Chamberlain's plan to awaken the nation to its imperial responsibilities. In October 2001, long before the dust had settled in lower Manhattan, a "beaming" Blair was captured in *The Sun* posing in Oman "shoulder to shoulder" with Corporal Kevin Lee, "a British soldier ready to put the boot into Osama bin Laden." Corporal Lee, a veteran of the previous Gulf War, was pictured sporting a "Gulf-War-vintage T-shirt bearing the slogan 'We Came, We Saw, We Kicked Ass.' " In between outing himself as a Newcastle United supporter and discussing army life with soldiers over chicken curry and strawberry ice cream, the prime minister, "standing in scorching heat in an open-necked shirt and khaki slacks" offered this diagnosis of the world's predicament on the brink of the invasion of Afghanistan: "What is at stake is whether we try to resolve the difference between people by negotiation or understanding—or let fanatics or extremists determine our fate. You the armed forces, are our front line in the struggle for freedom and justice. . . . We are also defending values about democracy, freedom, the ability to respect people of different faiths, races and creeds, and a belief that we will create a better world."[5]

Even through the filters of the Murdoch press, this outlook should be recognizable as an update of older themes. Its key features echo arguments in support of the legitimacy of European colonial expropriation that were first slyly made by John Locke and his seventeenth-century interlocutors. Locke, you may recall, saw that process of colonial conquest as a way to "improve" the world. He winked at the military projects of North America's colonial settlers and decried the lives of the country's savage occupants who were content to have their needs met by the hidden hand of nature rather than buy into the approved blend of industry and rationality that could secure a legal right to the land they had managed to occupy for centuries without conceiving it as private property. Both they and it needed to be improved, and the philosophers of England's emergent bourgeoisie were only too happy to take on these tasks.

Today, the point of view that makes the improvement of a resentful and unappreciative world by imperial powers into a matter of morals can call itself cosmopolitan. That designation is, of course, qualified by a continuing attachment to the idea that the national state should remain the primary institutional guarantor of political rights. These advocates of cosmopolitanism have become shy of the noble idea of world citizenship that has been traced back to the Cynics and Stoics and still proves attractive to many in an essentially Kantian, "enlightenment" form. Their brand of ethical imperialism is far more inclined to construct a different cosmopolitical agenda in the coalitional coming together of willing national states oriented by the goal of enforcing a desiderata of peace, privatization, and market mechanisms on a global scale. Existing versions of international law are not thought to provide adequate justification for this exercise in spreading civilization by force. The moralistic and humanitarian basis of this twenty-first century cosmopolitanism is uncomfortable with conventional notions of sovereignty that might obstruct its desire for increased moral and military reach. Where the need for improvement is most intense, bad or inadequate governance, even if it has won some sort of local political mandate, becomes vulnerable to the humanitarian case for political and military intervention. Under these circumstances, strict legality and moral legitimacy will conflict. When that happens, it is clear that it is legitimacy, established beyond the grasp of political institutions through moral and moralistic argument, that is likely to prove the victor. Shifting into nebulous moral argument rather than sticking strictly to grounded political criteria is also significant because it has sometimes provided alibis for the geopolitical interests of powerful countries that are not reciprocally vulnerable to the moral indictments of their own democratic lapses, which could be made by weaker national states or other political bodies for whom rights do not provide the main technique for addressing injustice.

Though its origins are much older, lying in the first phases of European expansion, this new armored cosmopolitanism has been built upon foundations supplied by enlightenment anthropology. It retains, for example, many of the ambiguities of that period with regard to the significance of racial difference. Secreted inside the dazzling rhetoric of universal inclusiveness and limitless variation within humankind, there is another pragmatic and hierarchical anthropology that can recognize a degree of injustice in imperial conquest but be comfortable nonetheless with the commonsense wisdoms that produce race as a deep fracture in culture, capacity, and experience.

Racial difference obstructs empathy and makes ethnocentrism inescapable. It becomes impossible even to imagine what it is like to be somebody else. We will see later on that, at the very same time, the powerful and pleasurable fantasy of transgressing that impassable boundary has started to circulate through the core of popular culture. Ethnic absolutism is a fashionable feature of the identity politics that makes the practice of substantive politics impossible. Instead, we are all sealed up inside our frozen cultural habits, and there seems to be no workable precedent for adopting a more generous and creative view of how human beings might communicate or act in concert across racial, ethnic, or civilizational divisions.

Solidarity Becomes Suspect

These days, much of what passes for radical and critical thought rests on the notion that the very aspiration toward translocal solidarity, community, and interconnection is tainted. This is because it is a symptom of imperial arrogance and the mainspring of a violent ethnocentrism, which wants to make everybody essentially the same and in doing so, make them all "western." That outcome identifies a great danger in humanity's being recast as a legion of clones. It cannot at present compete with a more popular alternative fantasy. This second option focuses not on individuals but on disciplined and homogenous collective groups. They too are represented as absolutely different from each other. The power of race and ethnicity is inflated in order to justify that projection. This scenario offers a basic choice between the hypersimilarity of clone identity (operating on several scales: race, nation, or ethnic group) or a different position, which abandons those forms of seriality in favor of a radically individualistic view of humanity that makes any collective identity arbitrary, transitional, and, most importantly, politically irrelevant.

There are many eloquent and powerful theoretical endorsements of this gloomy choice and the negative view of cross-cultural understanding and transnational solidarity that goes with it. Profound and disturbing forms of it are at stake in debates over the cultural legacies of genocide and mass death on and off the battlefield, as well as in twentieth-century discussions of memory, trauma, and the category of experience itself. My desire to understand its contemporary resonance led me back to Freud's sociological and historical work. Those essays, produced during the 1914–1918 war and prompted by his observations of the rise of Fascism, direct us to the fissures within rather than between civilizations and employ the idea of repression to make the relation of culture to civilization complex and antagonistic. His warning that "civilized man has exchanged a portion of his possibilities of happiness for a portion of security" seems remote from a situation in which politics has become saturated by the desire to merge security with happiness and engineer the latter by repetition through the machinery of info-war invented by his nephew Edward Bernays. However, a rereading of *Civilization and Its Discontents* (1929) confirms the enduring value of Freud's insights. Following an argument that the inclination to aggression is an instinctual disposition among human beings whose social interaction is driven by a "primary mutual hostility" that impedes our acquisition of civilization, he dismisses the biblical injunction to love thy neighbor as thyself. He sees that stricture as an impossible and damaging inflation, which can only bring unhappiness and devalue the idea of love: "A love that does not discriminate seems to me to forfeit part of its own value, by doing injustice to its object. . . . Not all men," he concludes, "are worthy of love."[6]

Freud's dense argument connects a discussion of the cost of striving in vain to live with supposedly intolerable difference with an explicit, though shallow consideration of the effects of racial hostility. His formulation of this problem is superficially mild. Love, rather than genial indifference, sets the standard, and it is, after all, only the neighbor and not the more demanding figures of the enemy and the stranger who is being brought within the sphere of this impossible request for tolerance with intimacy. His disenchanted pronouncements on the impossibility of undifferentiated love for one's fellow humans were a prelude to the observation that whole civilizations as well as individuals could enter periods of neurosis. That oblique comment on the interwar condition of Europe's political culture also provides a useful starting point for discussion of recent changes in the quality of political culture and society in the United States since the "war on terror" was launched.

A strong connection between racism and the failures of civilization is revealed in the discussions of anti-Semitism that pepper the text. The positive service done on behalf of civilization by the Jewish people who were massacred during the Middle Ages and have served more recently as what Freud calls "agents of economic discharge" in the world of the Aryan ideal is sarcastically introduced. The "narcissism of minor differences," the key term which describes the aggression of closely proximate and intimately familiar groups whose internal cohesion and solidarity are interleaved with an apparently disproportionate mutual hatred, is another invaluable element in this contribution. Though it does not explain the sources of aggression or help us distinguish the minor from the major, that concept does acknowledge the space in which the mechanisms of racism intervene to manage the reluctance of groups to concede their essential sameness.

I am not suggesting that the rise of Nazism and Fascism during the twentieth century can, any more than their contemporary resurgence, be adequately explained by the suggestion that they were somehow caused by racism alone. However, it is not fanciful to suppose that Freud had those historic developments in mind when he framed these speculations. His argument culminates in the recommendation that we need what he calls "a pathology of cultural communities." He is calling, in other words, for a particular form of inquiry directed at the psychological poverty and pathological character of groups that understand their collective life and fate in specifically cultural terms.

Many problems arise in simply extending his sense of the difficulties involved in exchanging security for happiness outward from an account of the social interaction between individuals into the different forms of analysis required to explain social relationships that exist between groups. However, I would like to align the critical exploration of racial discourse and its consequences with what I take to be the guiding spirit of Freud's advocacy in pursuit of the anatomization of cultural groups. It was focused initially by his presentation of the conflict between the social obligation to love one's fellow citizens and the unhappiness involved in the impossible attempt to do so, but the implications of this particular pathological pattern extend still further. They might certainly be made to include the production of national, racial, and ethnic groups as historical and political actors as well as to encompass a consideration of the openings that racism affords for the discharge of a "non-erotic aggressivity and destructiveness." These are outcomes that might otherwise appear baffling.

The fatalistic tone that arises from Freud's muted response to Fascism and his evident desire to interpret its popular appeal has been bolstered and reproduced by many acute and brilliant twentieth-century commentators. Claude Lévi-Strauss was another influential voice prepared to point out that, irrespective of its momentous rhetorical and emotional force, the idea of unbounded or universal humanity was a very recent invention associated historically with the great privilege of a life beyond the grip of scarcity. From my point of view, it would be more useful to see that this novel response derived from a confrontation with the inhumanity of the Fascist period and, in particular, with the governmental outcomes of racial science and hygiene.

Lévi-Strauss emphasizes that this unprecedented commitment to universal humanity has been unevenly distributed among humankind. Once again, in the context of an ambiguous but provocative meditation on the subjects of "race" and history, he argues that an unrealistic abolition of difference is entailed by the well-intentioned but empty refusal to define bounded community. Though it sounds noble, this refusal is, for him, a very dubious gesture. When it is combined with the introduction of temporality as the medium of differentiation, it has the unintended consequence of making everybody the same but then rearranging them in a historical sequence that rationalizes their differences and their conflicts by suggesting they are all in progressive motion toward the same ultimate destination. Some groups then represent the past of others, some are social and political adults while others are children. Their civilizations are advanced or backward. The binary "pep rally" logic of winners and losers is thereby instated on the geopolitical stage. The challenge of multiculturalism can be defined, on the other hand, in the idea of bringing these diverse groups into the same present and the project of fusing their horizons so that the possibility of a common future becomes conceivable. Antiracism can contribute explicitly to that goal.

Lévi-Strauss was determined to separate the issue of racial inequality from the different problem of cultural diversity with which it was becoming entangled. He does not identify the introduction of time as a medium of differentiation with the appearance of properly modern and scientific versions of race thinking during the nineteenth century or connect those changes with the colonial militarization of the national state that followed soon after. Instead, he conveys his general dissatisfaction with the way the idea of a world civilization is being used in discussions of what will succeed the genocidal attachment to race hierarchy revealed by Nazism. He discovers a more fruitful conception in a revised view of world civilization as what he calls "a world-wide coalition of cultures, each of which would preserve its own originality."[7] Those terms, "preservation" and "coalition," presuppose recognition of alterity, but he offers no insights into the operation of the tricky procedures involved in applying them. He seems to conceive of that recognition as a straightforward and unidirectional affair. We, on the other hand, are obliged to distinguish the compound formation on which he rests his hopes from the de facto dominance of the North American empire that has become a real prospect in the decade since Samuel Huntington first announced that it would be impossible to attain.

The challenge of being in the same present, of synchronizing difference and articulating cosmopolitan hope upward from below rather than imposing it downward from on high provides some help in seeing how we might invent conceptions of humanity that allow for the presumption of equal value and go beyond the issue of tolerance into a more active engagement with the irreducible value of diversity within sameness. There is another quite different idea of cosmopolitanism to be explored here. Its value to the politics of multiculturalism lies in its refusal of state-centeredness and in its attractive vernacular style. In a sharp contrast with the recipes for good governance that have been pronounced from up above, this variant might be described as a "vulgar" or "demotic" cosmopolitanism. This cosmopolitan attachment finds civic and ethical value in the process of exposure to otherness. It glories in the ordinary virtues and ironies—listening, looking, discretion, friendship—that can be cultivated when mundane encounters with difference become rewarding. The self-knowledge that can be acquired through the proximity to strangers is certainly precious but is no longer the primary issue. We might consider how to cultivate the capacity to act morally and justly not just in the face of otherness—imploring or hostile—but in response to the xenophobia and violence that threaten to engulf, purify, or erase it.

The opportunity for self-knowledge is certainly worthwhile, but, especially in turbulent political climates, it must take second place behind the principled and methodical cultivation of a degree of estrangement from one's own culture and history. That too might qualify as essential to a cosmopolitan commitment. This distancing can sound like a privilege and has sometimes been associated with the history of elites, but I am not convinced that it is inevitably tainted by those associations. Something like it is now a routine feature of the postmodern and postcolonial processes that condition metropolitan life: diaspora dispersal, mass immigration, military travel, tourism, and the revolution in global communications, to name just a few. It has also emerged fitfully in the reflections of modern intellectuals dissatisfied by the prospect of being forcibly attached by patriotism and nationalism to cultural and political formations that are wrong, unjust, evil, or misguided and therefore unrepresentative.

As he watched the destructive vortex of World War I suck in so much of what was precious and worth defending in European civilization, Freud lamented the failure of the civilized world to move beyond war as a means of settling its disputes. His essays from that time capture the flavor of the cosmopolitan response offered by powerless and disillusioned individuals who have cultivated a larger loyalty to civilization than their original national states could possibly contain or allow. He describes their predicament and connects it to the acquisition of a nonnational or transnational "fatherland" that can serve the disillusioned and estranged as a "museum" in which the very best and most meaningful elements of human culture might be stored for uplifting contemplation. In this relationship with worldly culture, nothing seems foreign to the disenchanted cosmopolitan who does not reproach "himself . . . for being a renegade towards his own nation and his beloved mother tongue." Freud addresses the cultural gap that opened up during wartime between those who were able to retain their larger loyalties and those whose "susceptibility to culture" was undone by the deception and emotional excitement of geopolitical conflicts that only became meaningful through restrictive, nationalist attachments. The result of this division was alienation from one's fellow citizens, but understanding how it had come about could make the inevitable disillusionment easier to bear:

> The state exacts the utmost degree of obedience and sacrifice from its citizens, but at the same time it treats them like children by an excess of secrecy and censorship upon news and expressions of opinion which leaves the spirits of those intellects it thus suppresses defenceless against every unfavourable turn of events and every sinister rumour. It absolves itself from guarantees and treaties by which it was bound to other states, and confesses shamelessly to its own rapacity and lust for power, which the private individual has then to sanction in the name of patriotism.[8]

The same kind of intuitive estrangement can be found in the work of many fugitives and refugees from Nazism. It culminates in a new way of being at home in the world through an active hostility toward national solidarity, national culture, and their privileging over other, more open affiliations.

Cosmopolitanism and the Planetary Mentality

It is important not to see this type of response as an exclusively twentieth-century phenomenon. This sort of thinking has appeared intermittently in a host of writers dotted through the grand tradition of reflection upon European modernity. It was woven into their ethical indictments of Europe's colonial adventures and their critiques of its political and economic inconsistencies and shortcomings since Montaigne's essay "On the Cannibals," where an ironic acknowledgment of one surprisingly wise stranger's alien mode of dress concluded a provocative exploration of problems we would come to know much later as the ethics of translation and the mechanics of interculture. Rather than recycling the ambiguities in the Kantian system to which I have already referred, I want to return to Montesquieu's satirical novel *Persian Letters*, which is invaluable as a source of clues as to the genealogy of these positions as well as for its example of what a healthier orientation toward the unsettling experience of exposure to otherness might add up to.

Montesquieu's refusal of orientalist fantasy and subtle reinscription of it in a critical anthropology of his own society also makes a number of more general points about the value of estrangement and the disabilities that arise from familiarity with ways of life that can only look odd and irrational to outsiders. His novel concerns the experience of two Persian travelers, Usbek and Ibben, who are transformed by their journey into the metropolitan center of France under the *ancien régime*. Their observations of European and Christian habits in the contested heart of modern Europe's emergent public world address topics from religion and science to ethics, happiness, and revolution. While they are absent from their own place of origin and belonging, specifically from the unfree space of the harem that Usbek rules as husband, sovereign, and proprietor, his wives organize an insurrection. They overthrow the eunuchs whom he has set to control them, take the lovers of their choice, and then, in the storm of their revolution, commit suicide in acts of autonomy that, if they seem politically threadbare, do overthrow his assumptions of mastery: "No: I may have lived in servitude, but I have always been free. I have amended your laws according to the laws of nature, and my mind has always remained independent." We can imagine that these defiant, modern words, drawn from the novel's conclusion, have been spoken by a wife on behalf of slaves everywhere. They do more than register Europe's apprehensions about its colonial adventures and anticipate the debate about master and slave which would follow. They also communicate the dimensions of a different universality that can only come into being where the colonial "contact zone" has been succeeded by more ordinary and perhaps more distinctively metropolitan forms of interaction with the strange and the alien.

The cosmopolitan position from which Montesquieu wrote suggests that imagining oneself as a stranger in a limited and creative sense might instructively be linked to actually becoming estranged from the cultural habits one is born to. This alienation was not for him a disadvantage; it is his anthropological and indeed ethical method. It cannot guarantee undistorted perception of the world but can still be used to show where overfamiliarity enters and taken-for-grantedness corrupts. His travelers' experiences establish that being a stranger can be invaluable as an opportunity to know the world better and to experience it in more complex and satisfying forms.

Montesquieu's enlightenment tale disguised its fictional character as a sequence of authentic letters. His imaginary alien visitors offered a scurrilous critical commentary on modern metropolitan life. The social and moral conventions of the day were subjected to the anthropological gaze of a stranger, which aimed to reintroduce France to itself and to suggest that critical knowledge of one's own culture and society can only arise from a carefully cultivated degree of estrangement. Similar issues enveloped the humorous antics of the comic figure Ali G, who for a year or two recently managed to encapsulate all the larger political moral debates over the character and direction of contemporary British social life. His appeal will be discussed in more detail later on. Here, it is worth appreciating that his fleeting triumph brought new life to some subversive eighteenth-century tactics. I'm sure that Ali G's highly educated creators knew that a sense of what it meant to be English was at stake in the timeliness of their jokes. No wonder then that the comedian who plays him, Sacha Baron-Cohen, concealed the political intelligence that guided his project by refusing to step outside of his character.

Ali G was as much at ease in the postcolonial city as Uzbek and Ibben had been in Montesquieu's Paris. To all of them, the metropolis provided a fragmented and stratified location in which cultures, histories, and structures of feeling previously separated by enormous distances could be found in the same place, the same time: school, bus, café, cell, waiting room, or traffic jam. The results of this proximity are not always harmonious, but every notion of culture as property is broken and dispersed by the swirling, vertiginous motion of the postcolonial world for which Ali was an unwitting spokesman.

It is not far-fetched to suggest that the huge amounts of energy that were wasted worrying about whether the Ali G character was a white Jew pretending to be black, a white Jew pretending to be a white pretending to be black, a white Jew pretending to be an Asian pretending to be black, and so on might have been better spent positioning his tactics in a proper historical and artistic sequence of strangers whose strangeness was functional and educative. It is telling that there were no similar discussions when Ali's author extended his repertoire to include the even more Montesquieuian figure of Borat the Khazakstani refugee.

Among his other great achievements, Montesquieu seems to have been among the first thinkers to suggest that we must learn to practice a systematic form of disloyalty to our own local civilization if we seek either to understand it or to interact equitably with others formed elsewhere. Adrienne Rich's luminous contribution to analyzing this problem reminds us that his argument has been extended by several generations of Feminist political reflection to include those other Others formed nearby but kept out of sight behind the veils of cultural and political segregation: "What has stopped me short, what fuses my anger now, is that we were told we were utterly different, *that the difference between us must be everything, must be determinative, that from that difference we each must turn away; that we must also flee from our alikeness.*"[9] Today, the women's movement to which Rich's angry words were addressed has faded and disappeared. The new obligation to grasp the global workings of imperial domination has been placed upon would-be world citizens. It intervenes to deny us the freedoms that Montesquieu and Baron-Cohen have enjoyed: either to invent the alien culture from which covert judgments of our own social order could be made or to project our critique of existing arrangements onto the aliens around us. In our circumstances, these ironic exercises in anthropological thinking have become little more than a joke.

From Ali G to Multicultural Democracy

All this means that though I am drawing inspiration from Freud's attempt to link the impossible injunction to love the unfamiliar with a speculative and critical account of the development of pathological intercommunal relations, I want to dispute his explicit rejection of the demand to practice an undifferentiated attitude toward friends and enemies, intimates and strangers, alike. I want to suggest that politics can be invented and practiced outside of Carl Schmitt's militaristic distinctions. Instead of accepting in the name of realism that his Manichaean system governs all our options, I want to explore ways in which the ordinary cosmopolitanism, so characteristic of postcolonial life might be sustained and even elevated. I would like it to be used to generate abstract but nonetheless invaluable commitments in the agonistic development of a multicultural democracy that Freud and the others cannot be expected to have been able to foresee.

I am obliged to link this historic possibility to a different understanding of the postmodern than the one that is defined through hyperindividualism and consumerism. This postmodern predicament is not driven by consumerist impulses but by a critique of them, not by unchecked capitalism but by a sense that nature enforces limits on the human capacity to remake and transform the world. It does not reveal itself in the composition of identity from "the fragmentary remains of old cultures and religions." It can be approached through the translocal impact of political ideologies, social relations, and technological changes that have fostered a novel sense of interdependence, simultaneity, and mutuality in which the strategic and economic choices made by one group on our planet may be connected in a complex manner with the lives, hopes, and choices of others who may be far away.

This approach has deep roots in the varieties of cosmopolitan solidarity proposed by the generation of DuBois (born 1868) and Gandhi (born 1869) and enacted in the national-liberation and decolonization struggles they anticipated and led. Its resurgent appeal was captured some years ago by the slogan "act locally, think globally," and since then, the same insubordinate spirit has lent emotional and ethical energy to trans-local movements against racism and inequality around health, disease, and the environment. This transmodern dissidence is increasingly connected to the emergence of an anticapitalist culture that aims to make resistance to neoliberalism as global as capital itself has become.

A number of different elements can be identified here. All of them are associated with a fundamental change in the way that our planet is itself apprehended and understood, beyond the cosmography of Newtonian mechanisms and outside of the geopolitical sensibilities of the imperial age that were distilled so neatly by Hannah Arendt in her citation of Cecil Rhodes' famous desire to "annex the planets" if he could.[10] The last third of the twentieth century saw our world becoming a different kind of object, approached through a geo-piety that operates on an earthly scale and is not oriented by fundamental concern for the sovereign territory of national states. Images of the Earth photographed from outside its orbit by the Apollo spacecraft in 1972 have emerged as the emblem or signature of this novel planetary consciousness. The icy New York demonstrations that contributed to the day of rolling worldwide protest against the war in Iraq on 15 February 2003 involved hundreds of dark blue flags bearing the iconic imprint of NASA photograph AS17-22727. This is a striking image of the Earth isolated, whole, delicate, and centerless. It was sometimes, though by no means always, captioned with the simple phrase "not in our name."

Carl Schmitt, who reckoned himself to be a historian of these perceptual and geocultural shifts, can once again be a valuable guide. His interest in the racial and civilizational patterns of world history led him to see that the "early-modern" expansion of European powers involved a revolutionary change of scale, which had generated profound economic, philosophical, and geopolitical consequences. The Earth itself would be represented differently as a result:

> The great changes in the geographic image of our planet are but a superficial aspect of the deep-going mutation, [as] suggested by the phrase "spatial revolution," so rich in consequences. What by turn has been called the rational superiority of the Europeans, the European spirit and "Western Rationalism" has had an irresistible impact ever since. It extended the nations of Western and Central Europe, destroyed the medieval forms of human community, set up new states, fleets and armies, invented new machines, and submitted to its will the non-European peoples. To the latter it gave the choice of adopting European civilization or be reduced to mere colonies of the former.[11]

It is well known that the institution of this belligerent transmodernity ended medieval conceptions of locally bounded life and was connected to displacement of the Earth from the center of the cosmos. It was succeeded in the eighteenth century by the revolutionary upheaval that produced anthropology and introduced "man" as an object of knowledge and power. This time, another decisive change of scale, which Foucault tentatively christens "the analytic of finitude," can be identified here. Once again, it was bound up with ethical matters, and once again, *Persian Letters* provides an invaluable illustration of the difference this connection could make. Montesquieu's ordinary cosmopolitanism showed how a shift in the perception of the Earth onto a cosmic scale was connected not only to questions of human universality, agency, difference, and comparison but also to pressing moral matters. This is most clear in the arguments for the decriminalization of suicide that are famously voiced by Usbek in letter 76"

> When my soul shall be separated from my body, will there be any less order in the universe? Do you believe that any new combination will be less perfect or less dependent upon general laws, or that the universe will have lost something, or that the works of God will be less great or, rather, less immense? Do you think that my body, having

become a blade of wheat, a worm, or a piece of lawn, would be changed into a work less worthy of nature, and would my soul, freed of everything terrestrial, become less sublime? All such ideas . . . originate in our pride alone. We do not realise our littleness, and in spite of everything we want to count for something in the universe, play a part, be a person of importance."

The universality that comes into view from the cosmic angle must submit to the stern ethical tests that suicide, incest, and divorce provide for enlightened rationality. Montesquieu's musings on this theme bring to mind the contribution of Giacomo Leopardi, who became exercised about the changing character of the act of suicide not just because he understood that a cosmic perspective transformed our sense of the value of life but also because he could see that the historical and sociological changes of his time (1798–1837) had begun alter its meaning.

In Leopardi, cosmic sensibility was linked once again to a profound despair. He was fascinated by the Copernican revolution and has Copernicus appear in one of his richest *Moral Tales* to announce the end of human uniqueness in a light-hearted dialogue with the Sun. Leopardi's writing transmits the same inconsolable, tragicosmic sense of human triviality into the nineteenth century, where it endowed a negative, misanthropic hope in his modernist grasp of "the nullity of things" and "the inevitability of unhappiness." This combination was starkly evident in his view of slavery and contributed to a humanist outlook quite different from the triumphalist tone of official humanisms. This cosmopolitanism was born from centering subjectivity on suffering rather than sovereignty or autonomy. It reveals no misplaced faith in automatic progress and retreats from the world of formal or institutional politics into the areas of ethical judgment where its theodicy can be revealed. The resulting collision spoke directly to the immoral institution of racial slavery and the dubious extension of European powers into the rest of the planet. His notebooks included this aphorism on the relationship between race and philosophy:

> In the present century, black people are believed to be totally different from whites in race and origin, yet totally equal to them with regard to human rights. In the sixteenth century, when blacks were thought to come from the same roots and to be of the same family as whites, it was held, most of all by Spanish theologians, that with regard to rights blacks were by nature and Divine Will greatly inferior to us. In both centuries, blacks have been bought and sold and made to work in chains under the whip. Such is ethics; and such is the extent to which moral beliefs have anything to do with actions.[12]

Something of the same hopeful despair marks the postmodern planetary consciousness I am invoking here as a stimulus to multiculture and a support for anti-racist solidarity. It relies on a reimagining of the world which is as extensive and profound as any of the revolutionary changes in the perception and representation of space and matter that preceded it. The world becomes not a limitless globe, but a small, fragile, and finite place, one planet among others with strictly limited resources that are allocated unequally. This is not the globalized mindset of the fortunate, unrestricted traveler or some other unexpected fruit of heavily insulated postscarcity and indifferent overdevelopment. It is a critical orientation and an oppositional mood triggered by comprehension of the simple fact that environmental and medical crises do not stop at national boundaries and by a feeling that the sustainability of our species is itself in question. This break with modern political consciousness increasingly includes a well-developed antipathy to the destructive global workings of "turbo-capitalism."

The change of scale tied into this "Apollonian" view of the whole world promotes a novel sense of our relationship with the biosphere. It supports an appreciation of nature as a common condition of our imperiled existence, resistant to commodification and, on some level, deeply incompatible with the institution of private property that made land into a commodity and legitimized chattel slavery. The most obvious illustrations of what this mentality looks like when it is translated into cosmopolitan action are the worldwide battles against AIDS and HIV and the struggle to secure free access to the water of which our bodies are largely composed. The same approach surfaces in many campaigns to resist corporate control of the substance of life itself, especially in the form of genetically modified seeds, as well as the global resistance to the privatization and copyrighting of natural materials with commercial possibilities, which has linked the colonization of territory and human beings with the colonization of all of life. "Another world is possible" is the latest slogan that has been chosen to foster this cosmopolitan outlook. It connotes neither a humanism in the classical sense of that term nor an unsteady affiliate of the liberal, midcentury Cold War mutations of that ideology. This is a planetary consciousness of the tragedy, fragility, and brevity of indivisible human existence that is all the more valuable as a result of its openness to the damage done by racisms. It is not, however, a matter of reading a new genealogy of "race" refracted in the prisms of humanism, of speaking belatedly back to Descartes' specifications of the human subject. This consciousness is not the other side of his anxious apprehension that he might in some other order have been born Chinese or a Cannibal.

Translocal Solidarity: The Elephant in the Room

Like many young Britons of my generation, I was given George Orwell's autobiographical essay "Shooting an Elephant" to read in secondary school. Midway between the end of World War II and the end of the century, it had become a valued part of our English curriculum. We were given it to criticize practically by faithful Leavisite teachers in order to learn how to write English in the proper manner. There were a number of other possible transactions in our encounter with that text, which was not only a means of learning English but of learning to be English in a worldly mode that remains both distinctive and valuable. That awareness was premised on a strong sense of the absurdity and destructiveness of the empire and the toll it had taken of the country's moral and humanitarian stock. Orwell's essay captured these feelings comprehensively:

> Suddenly I realised that I should have to shoot the elephant after all
> . . . it was at this moment, as I stood there with the rifle in my hands
> that I grasped the hollowness, the futility of the white man's domin-
> ion in the East. Here was I, the white man with his gun, standing in
> front of an unarmed native crowd—seemingly the leading actor in
> the piece; but in reality I was only an absurd puppet pushed to and
> fro by the will of those yellow faces behind. I perceived in this
> moment that when the white man turns tyrant it is his own freedom
> he destroys. He becomes a sort of hollow posing dummy. . . . He
> wears a mask and his face grows to fit into it. I had got to shoot the
> elephant.[13]

The lesson was repeated in my successive experiences of reading Orwell and placing his legacies in the genealogies of twentieth-century socialism and anarchism. His combination of anti-imperialism and patriotic attachment to a uniquely English ecology of belonging is a more complex, more disturbing, and, these days, more important quarry. It has not been dealt with properly in the deluge of autobiographical investigations that swamped the centenary of his birth.

The nature of Orwell's cosmopolitan affiliations—it seems inappropri-ate at that point in the twentieth century to use the overburdened word identity—was made clear not only by the decision to risk his life fighting against the Phalange in Spain but also by his determination to include the colonies and their consequences—political and economic as well as cul-tural—in the dissident inventory of British life he was making. This vision-ary commitment was also tied into a worldly consciousness that was artic-ulated in strict harmony with Orwell's parochial attachments to England's distinctive environment. His celebrated essay "Some Thoughts on the Common Toad" concludes, for example, with an appreciation of spring and the cycle of seasons, which is felt to be all the more welcome and special because it is something that the powers of authoritarian governments cannot regulate: "So long as you are not actually ill, hungry, frightened or immured in prison or a holiday camp, spring is still spring. The atom bombs are piling up in factories, the police are prowling through the cities, the lies are streaming from the loudspeakers, but the earth is still going around the sun, and neither dictators nor the bureaucrats, deeply as they disapprove of the process, are able to prevent it." This cosmic outlook should not be misinterpreted as a narrow brand of internationalism. It is explicit in its rejection of race and in its embrace of the empire's global reach. These qualities promote a more extensive and intimate conception of solidarity than internationalism can accommodate:

> What we always forget is that the overwhelming bulk of the British proletariat does not live in Britain, but in Asia and Africa. It is not in Hitler's power, for instance to make a penny an hour a normal industrial wage; it is perfectly normal in India, and we are at great pains to keep it so. . . . It is quite common for an Indian coolie's leg to be thinner than the average Englishman's arm. And there is nothing racial in this, for well-fed members of the same races are of normal physique; it is due to simple starvation. This is the system which we all live on and which we denounce when there seems to be no danger of its being altered.[14]

Orwell's view of the Empire and its geographically dispersed proletariat identified aspects of politics and economics in which the interests of domestic and overseas subjects of the crown diverged. This unusual outlook was forged by his experience as an imperial functionary in Burma, where he served in the police. His 1931 essay "A Hanging" provides a good place to start making an assessment of how that formative experience drew him into the humanistic outlook which anchors his impatient universalism and is directed sharply against the injustice and inequality of the empire's racial dominion. That essay describes an execution at which he has to officiate. The grim proceedings are disrupted by the intrusion of a stray dog, which, like Emmanuel Levinas's canine pal Bobby in his essay "The Name of a Dog, or Natural Rights," inadvertently humanizes the condemned man by refusing to respect the false gravity that Britain's remote government has invested in this exercise of its overarching power. Orwell's nameless dog—"half Airedale, half pariah"—rushes up to the prisoner and "jumping up tried to lick his face." The proximity of the canine brings some important dimensions of militant, anti-imperial humanity into focus. That change is clarified for Orwell as he watches the prisoner step aside to avoid a puddle in his path toward the gallows. At that point, the disenchanted colonial policeman is not only able to grasp the common humanity that binds him shamefully to the prisoner's fate but to understand the absolute injustice involved in putting him to death: "I saw the unspeakable wrongness, of cutting a life short when it is in full tide. This man was not dying, he was alive just as we were alive . . . he and we were a party of men walking together, seeing hearing, feeling, understanding the same world; and in two minutes, with a sudden snap, one of us would be gone—one mind less, one world less." It is important, too, that at the critical moment, Orwell turned inward on the body. He moves inside it to consider the functioning of the prisoner's organs, his bowels, skin, nails, and unimpaired sensorium. This vital humanity, which can only be realized in the overthrow of injustice, directs attention away from all anthropology and toward the "bestial floor" of human being in the body, in particular to ordinary experiences of sickness and suffering. These issues returned some years later in Winston Smith's shocking confrontation with his own emaciated and sickly body after he has been broken in the Ministry Of Love and, memorably, in another essay, "How the Poor Die," which reflects upon Orwell's 1929 experience of being hospitalized in Paris. There, it was class-bound governmental power that touched the bodies of the poor with a similar pointless brutality and made their corpses into disgusting pieces of refuse. Orwell explains that his understanding of death and power was transformed in an encounter with "the first dead European" he had seen. "I had seen dead men before, but always Asiatics and usually people who had died violent deaths." The "impersonality of a place where every day people are dying among strangers" suggests that the routine injustices of the colonial space have counterparts in the working of institutions closer to home, in the public wards of France, if not in English hospitals.

I think Orwell's example matters now not just because his work should be placed at the source of those traditions of dissenting cultural reflection and analysis that operate under the sign of "Cultural Studies" but because his insight and courage are wrongly and routinely recuperated in traditions of political culture that are far too nation-centered and narrowly patriotic. His experiences in Burma, Spain, and Paris have not been made useful in the same ways as his peregrinations inside Britain. His itinerancy has attracted a hostility that goes beyond the routine sectarianism of the left. It becomes an issue of how conceptions of culture, agency, and solidarity that are not overwhelmingly national in character contend with those that can only operate within the closed world of the national state.

Toward the end of *Culture and Society*, Raymond Williams dismisses Orwell with the observation that what he calls "the paradox of exile" supplied an interpretative key to the enigma of his political stance. For Williams, Orwell's "vagrancy" trapped him some distance short of the community his socialism craved but could not realize. He argues that Orwell's humane instincts broke down under the resulting pressure and disintegrated into nothing but a "caustic dust." Williams' expression of his criticisms in terms of Orwell's exilic suspicion of community is directly relevant. Even if we accept this contentious diagnosis, there is in Williams a significant reticence about the other possible elements of this peculiar cultural transaction. What, after all, might the vagrant and exile have gained by their separation from the cozy comforts of the national community, even in its worthy oppositional pattern? For brevity's sake, I shall say only that Orwell might be thought of as having traded the dubious benefits of his imperial Brit nationality for a rare opportunity to connect with and even understand the whole world. This is not, as we saw Freud argue, a devaluation of love, but its transmutation into the fragile, emergent substance of vital planetary humanism. With this example in mind, we might want to consider the moral and political challenges of some contemporary events in a manner similar to Orwell's solidarity with democracy in Spain. The spirit of connection discovered there might even be recycled and employed to transform our understanding of how translocal solidarity can work so that we are more informed, more sensitive, less intimidated, and more likely to act.

The growing band of people who opt to bear active witness to distant suffering and even to place their lives at risk in many parts of the world as human shields thankfully represent the undoing of identity politics. Their practical answer to imperialism, racism, and the narcissism of minor differences mobilizes the invaluable solidarity of the slightly different. Its immediate, tactical value derives from the fact that as far as unjust colonial force is concerned, its Gandhian practitioners appear to be different from the infrahuman objects of brutality and arbitrary power that they set out to shield. Theirs is a translocal commitment to the alleviation of suffering and to the practical transfiguration of democracy which is incompatible with racism and ethnic absolutism. It is only racism that acknowledges the difference between their rights-bearing bodies and those of the rights-less people they protect by their presence. These gestures of solidarity proceed from the assumption that translation will be good enough to make the desired experiential, political, and ethical leap. Purposive vagrancy and exile, albeit in temporary forms, are again the order of the day. Once more, suffering rather than autonomy and self-possession has been located in the center of the public culture of an info-war quite different from the industrial conflicts in which Orwell, Fanon, and the rest took part as soldiers. Today the vagrants and exiles need no longer be combatants. They are more likely to be useful in the different role of nonviolent witnesses taking a calculated risk in the interest of peace and other cosmopolitan goals which, place war in the past as a way to solve human conflicts. Commitments to truth and open communication are anchored in and addressed to a consciousness of humankind that is defined on one side by a sense of the mutability of life and on the other by its singularity and continuity. The force of this gesture in the postcolonial present derives not from any misplaced romances with the murderous offspring of military technology but from an instructive and humble confrontation with the bloody human consequences of awesome imperial power. Where the lives of natives, prisoners and enemies are abject and vulnerable, they must be shielded by others, endowed with those more prestigious, rights-bearing bodies that can inhibit the brutal exercise of colonial governance.

Cosmopolitan solidarity from below and afar has been a notable feature of the global response to the Al-Aqsa intifada in Palestine. The mobilizing power of the Internet is evident in a striking movement of people from numerous countries into the territories occupied by Israel. They are determined to place themselves between the vulnerable victims of the occupation and the military firepower of the Israeli army. As we approach the end of this discussion of contemporary cosmopolitics, we should consider the motivation of these people and their accomplishments in the service of planetary humanism and global multiculture. Their acts of solidarity articulate a practical riposte to the despairing twentieth-century voices that wanted to discredit this sort of gesture by arguing that the openness and undifferentiated love from which it derives is tainted, ignoble, and unpolitical.

Tom Hurndall was a twenty-one-year-old man from North London who was shot in the head by the Israeli army on 11 April 2003 in the town of Rafah, close to the Egyptian border. He lay comatose, on a life-support machine at the Royal Free Hospital with severe brain damage until he died in January 2004. In an illuminating interview about the circumstances of his shooting, his mother Jocelyn provided some important clues as to her son's decision to move unarmed, as an act of solidarity and witness, into a zone of conflict: "Tom wanted to experience everything; he threw himself at life. He had gone to Israel to see a world outside his own. . . . He wanted to understand and feel at first hand what civilians were suffering in Palestine. He wanted to find the truth behind the propaganda, seek out injustices. . . . Tom went to Gaza to expose injustice. I profoundly respect the fact that he sought to make a difference. Somewhere along the line he decided to value life, not just his own, but those around him."[15] These impulses toward experience, suffering, injustice and truth seem characteristic of worldly, cosmopolitical activism. Jocelyn Hurndall's words also suggest an implicit critique of life in the overdeveloped world, which sounds as though it has been emptied of the varieties of experience her son desired and of the opportunity to make a real difference. The callous shooting of young people like Tom Hurndall exemplifies the eloquence and the limitations of individual acts of solidarity. By highlighting the discrepancy between assaulting nonlocals and the more routine assaults on the indigenous population, the international movement of witnesses and shields seeks to initiate a different humanitarian scheme or somatic economy in which all lives are seen to be equally precious and worth caring for. It should be emphasized that the implications of this and other similar cases cannot be confined to Israel alone. Once the colonial authorities revise and extend the category of infrahumanity to encompass anyone who is foolish enough to side with the insurgent locals, their fate must also represent a test of the democratic and judicial institutions of the incomer's country of origin. In Britain, the Hurndall family's modest and reasonable demand for government support in their pursuit of the truth about Tom's shooting has so far gone unheard. His mother reveals that when she and her husband returned to Rafah to visit the place where he had been shot, they too found themselves being fired upon by Israeli soldiers despite the fact that the troops had "been warned three times of their approach in a clearly marked British Embassy Range Rover."

The case of Rachel Corrie, another member of the international solidarity movement active in the Gaza strip, is rather better known.[16] She was a twenty-three-year-old U.S. citizen crushed by an Israeli army bulldozer on 16 March 2003 as she attempted to prevent the machine from demolishing a home in the same area of the Gaza strip where Hurndall was later shot. In Rachel Corrie's case, we do not have to rely on her parents' views in order to gain access to her thoughts and feelings about risking her life in defense of the weak and the vulnerable. Her own writing about her choices, in the form of e-mails to her family, is readily available and still circulates widely as part of the cosmopolitan remembrance of her death made possible by the new technology. The translation problems she encountered seem to have arisen more in her communication with her disbelieving parents than in her real-time interaction with her Palestinian hosts:

When that explosive detonated yesterday it broke all the windows in the family's house. I was in the process of being served tea and playing with two small babies. I am having a hard time right now. Just feel sick to my stomach a lot from being doted on all the time, very sweetly, by people who are facing doom. . . . Honestly, a lot of the time the sheer kindness of the people here, coupled with the overwhelming evidence of the willful destruction of their lives, makes it seem unreal to me. I really can't believe that something like this can happen in the world without a bigger outcry about it. It really hurts me, again, like it has hurt me in the past, to witness how awful we can allow the world to be. I felt after talking to you that you didn't completely believe me. I think it's actually good that you don't, because I do believe pretty much above all else in the importance of independent critical thinking.[17]

"How awful we can allow the world to be." Her phrase merits repetition for the lucidity with which it brings collective responsibility, planetary consciousness, and the horrors of imperial injustice into contact with one another. Anybody inclined to dismiss these protests and acts of solidarity as trivial should consider the fact that, in this case, the occupying power certainly does not regard them in that light. A memorial service for Rachel two days after her death was disrupted by the Israeli army, who fired tear gas at mourners and bullets over their heads. The scene was described by Joe Smith, another young American with the International Solidarity Movement: "They started firing tear gas and blowing smoke, then they fired sound grenades. After a while it got hectic so we sat down. Then the tank came over and shot in the air. . . . It scared a lot of Palestinians, especially the shooting made a lot of them run and the tear gas freaked people out. But most us stayed. . . . I don't think it was deliberate but it was pretty insensitive."[18]

We will see in the next chapter that open communication and solidarity from below have been answered by other cosmopolitical responses, directed downward by government. Their inspiration lies in a proposed revival of imperialism. It is no longer a source of guilt. It has been revised and rendered newly benign, progressive, and liberal. Like the "culturally appropriate" meals which we are told have been served out to U.S. prisoners at Camp Delta, this new approach to imperial power will mediate the conflict of civilizations that gets expressed in geopolitical relationships between postmodern and premodern states, overdeveloped and frozen economic zones.[19] Political conflicts arising from the latest phases of globalization are thus resolved into theories that promote the self-conscious rebirth of imperial relations. The principles of armored sover-eignty established during the nineteenth century will, of course, be mod-ified in favor of a new geometry of dependency and supposedly benevo-lent but firm, unyielding power that will secure the future order of the world. These perilous conditions and proposals make the cultivation of cosmopolitan disloyalty and the practice of systematic estrangement from the over-integrated culture of belligerent national states imperative. We will discover in the next chapter that some of this work is already spontaneously underway.

Part Two Albion

3   "Has It Come to This?"

Tales of heroism by the brave pilots of Spitfires and Hurricanes were
important to my postwar childhood. Their anti-Nazi action established
one dimension of my moral universe. Yet, when the World War II air-
planes thundered overhead during the pageantry that attended the Queen
Mother's burial in 2002, it was impossible not to wonder why that particular mythic moment of national becoming and community has been
able to endure and retain such a special grip on Britain's culture and self-
understanding. Why are those martial images—the battle of Britain, the
Blitz, and the war against Hitler—still circulating and, more importantly,
still defining the nation's finest hour? How is it that their potency can be

undiminished by the passage of time, and why do they alone provide the touchstone for the desirable forms of togetherness that are used continually to evaluate the chaotic, multicultural present and find it lacking?

Any worthwhile explanation for Britain's postmodern nationalism has to be complex enough to answer those questions. It must also be able to acknowledge that exceptionally powerful feelings of comfort and compensation are produced by the prospect of even a partial restoration of the country's long-vanished homogeneity. Repairing that aching loss is usually signified by the recovery or preservation of endangered whiteness—and the exhilarating triumph over chaos and strangeness which that victory entails. If this partial explanation is to become valid, it will have to account for how Britain's nationalism has interfaced with its racism and its xenophobia, but there is another interpretative challenge here. We need to know how the warm glow that results from the nation's wholesome militarism has combined pleasurably with the unchallenging moral architecture of a Manichaean world in which a number of dualistic pairings—black and white, savage and civilized, nature and culture, bad and good—can all be tidily superimposed upon one another. We will have to consider the pleasures that result from the experience of being happy, glorious, and victorious in a setting where the nation's characteristic ethnic blend of luck, pluck, and resilience can be identified and affirmed. Revisiting the feeling of victory in war supplies the best evidence that Britain's endangered civilization is in progressive motion toward its historic completion.

These distinctive combinations of sentiment and affect result in the anti-Nazi war being invoked even now. This is done so that Brits can know who we are as well as who we were and then become certain that we are still good while our uncivilized enemies are irredeemably evil. However, it is not obvious how and why the country's downbeat martial values still make sense to generations for whom the war itself is more myth and fantasy than memory. Political citations of World War II in pursuit of other more recent ends—the reconquest of the Falklands or the overthrow of Saddam Hussein—have stretched official anti-Fascist history so thin that it cannot possibly accomplish all the important cultural work it is increasingly relied upon to do. An uncertain generation for whom all knowledge of the conflict arrives on very long loops, usually via Hollywood, is still required to use expensively manufactured surrogate memory of World War II as the favored means to find and even to restore an ebbing sense of what it is to be English. Under these conditions, it has become instructive to ask why that war above all can connect people to the fading core of a culture and a history that is confronting a loss of certainty about its own distinctive content and its noble world mission. After all, the United Kingdom has been in plenty of other wars since the great triumph of 1945. Its troops have been dispatched to fight in the Netherlands East Indies, Palestine, Malaya, Korea, Kenya, Suez, Cyprus, Oman and Muscat, Brunei and Borneo, Saudi Arabia and Aden, Dofar, Ireland, the Falklands, the Persian Gulf, and then the Balkans. None of those conflicts—even the chronic warfare in Northern Ireland and the functional immediacy of Mrs. Thatcher's Falklands victory—can command a comparable ideological and mythological space. Scale, duration, and the remoteness of some of these battlefields from the homeland are insufficient explanations of why these conflicts have largely disappeared from view. The historical and conceptual problems they raise become more complex once we appreciate that the totemic power of the great anti-Nazi war seems to have increased even as its veterans have died out. On the other hand, the mysterious evacuation of Britain's postcolonial conflicts from national consciousness has become a significant cultural and historical event in its own right. Those forgotten wars have left significant marks on the body politic, but the memory of them appears to have been collapsed into the overarching figuration of Britain at war against the Nazis, under attack, yet stalwart and ultimately triumphant. That image, produced with apparent spontaneity from below and sometimes engineered politically from above by crown and government, has underpinned the country's unstable post-1945 settlement. It is addressed to what has become a perennial crisis of national identity, which lately reached a notable point of transition and decision in popular resistance to joining the U.S. invasion of Iraq and the debate over the terms upon which that special but dubious alliance with George Bush's superpower should now proceed.

Cultures of Melancholia and the Pathology of Greatness

I think that there is something neurotic about Britain's continued citation of the anti-Nazi war. Making it a privileged point of entry into national identity and self-understanding reveals a desire to find a way back to the point where the national culture—operating on a more manageable scale of community and social life—was, irrespective of the suffering involved in the conflict, both comprehensible and habitable. That memory of the country at war against foes who are simply, tidily, and uncomplicatedly evil has recently acquired the status of an ethnic myth. It explains not only how the nation remade itself through war and victory but can also be understood as a rejection or deferral of its present problems. That process is driven by the need to get back to the place or moment before the country lost its moral and cultural bearings. Neither the appeal of homogeneity nor the antipathy toward immigrants and strangers who represent the involution of national culture can be separated from that underlying hunger for reorientation. Turning back in this direction is also a turning away from the perceived dangers of pluralism and from the irreversible fact of multiculture.

The immediate roots of this situation reside in the way that Britain snatched a wider cultural and psychological defeat from the jaws of its victory over Hitlerism in 1945. I want to show that since then the life of the nation has been dominated by an inability even to face, never mind actually mourn, the profound change in circumstances and moods that followed the end of the empire and consequent loss of imperial prestige. That inability has been intertwined with the apprehension of successive political and economic crises, with the gradual breakup of the United Kingdom, with the arrival of substantial numbers of postcolonial citizen-migrants, and with the shock and anxiety that followed from a loss of any sense that the national collective was bound by a coherent and distinctive culture. Once the history of the empire became a source of discomfort, shame, and perplexity, its complexities and ambiguities were readily set aside. Rather than work through those feelings, that unsettling history was diminished, denied, and then, if possible, actively forgotten. The resulting silence feeds an additional catastrophe: the error of imagining that postcolonial people are only unwanted alien intruders without any substantive historical, political, or cultural connections to the collective life of their fellow subjects.

These extraordinary failures have obstructed the arterial system of Britain's political body in many ways. They deserve the proper name "postimperial melancholia" in order simultaneously to underline this syndrome's links with the past and its pathological character. This is a complex ailment with multiple symptoms that build upon and divert earlier patterns of imperial melancholy from which they make a decisive break. An older, more dignified sadness that was born in the nineteenth century should be sharply distinguished from the guilt-ridden loathing and depression that have come to characterize Britain's xenophobic responses to the strangers who have intruded upon it more recently.

Matthew Arnold helped to create the special "ethnic" space between Hebraism and Hellenism from which the country's Victorian racial destiny could be divined. By staging his famous poetic reflections on Britain's modern predicament at the frontier of Dover Beach, where today's asylum seekers still fear to tread, he made it clear that proximity to the alien presence of the French had helped to concentrate his mind with regard to the

[handwritten marginal note: postimperial melancholia]

country's historic responsibilities as well as its relationship to the classical world that had supplied the template for its global imperium. The historic mission to civilize and uplift the world was England's unavoidable destiny, but he sensed that it would bring neither comfort nor happiness. That imperial mission re-created the national community in a modern form but then drew it immediately into a terrible web of war and suffering, polluting its beautiful dreams, confusing and destabilizing it. For Arnold, the unchanging cliffs of England were glimmering and vast when compared to an ephemeral gleam of light visible on the nearby French coast. The distinctive island ecology of land and sea were operating on a geological tempo to which he gives the reader access. With the right dosage of Hellenic inspiration, the landscape/seascape could not only produce a deep geo-piety but also speak uniquely to the country's modern predicament and, of course, to the difficult position of the poet who bore a resigned witness to it. His apprehensions were aligned with those of the larger social body, but, as he heard and felt the shingle start to move beneath his feet, he opted to turn away from those public concerns and seek consolation in the private and intimate places where romantic love and fidelity could offset the worst effects of warfare, turbulence, and vanished certitude. The accompanying inward turn was a defensive gesture, and it was morally justifiable only when it promoted a self-conscious struggle with the historic sources of the tendency to become sad and pensive in the face of the empire's demanding geopolitical responsibilities.

We can say that Arnold's articulate melancholy was shaped by the culture of that empire in its emergent phase. It combined with and was complemented by the older melancholy of the poor, the expropriated, the empressed and the abjected which is still remembered in the folk music of England. An altogether different pattern became visible once the imperial system shifted into undeniable decline. Victorian melancholy started to yield to melancholia as soon as the natives and savages began to appear and make demands for recognition in the empire's metropolitan core. The change was complete when the limits of the political project involved in subordinating colonial peoples were communicated to their apprehensive racial betters by baffling ingratitude and a stubborn appetite for independence. At home, a novel conception of where the boundaries of British culture would fall was contoured by a new arrangement in which immigration, war, and national identity began to challenge class hierarchy as the most significant themes from which the national identity would be assembled. Until very recently, even the horrible shock of the First World War, which engulfed thousands and thousands of colonial soldiers, was recovered and preserved in an exclusionary form as a wholly private or domestic matter from which nonwhites were shut out by the force of the class conflicts that bound authentic Britons to each other in the manmade storm of military absurdity that made their divided lives expendable.

The end of external hostilities demanded a new map of the nation's internal fractures and divisions. The conflict between Celts and Anglo-Saxons was no longer adequate to the task of managing the inflow of aliens and their disruptive presence in the cities. Paul Foot drew attention long ago to the xenophobic populism swirling around the passage of the 1919 Aliens Act. He cites a powerful speech made in the House of Commons by Josiah Wedgewood, who set standards that today's Labour members of parliament have clearly been unable to maintain:

> Generally speaking, aliens are always hated by the people of this country. Usually speaking, there has been a mob which has been opposed to them, but that mob has always had leaders in high places. The Flemings were persecuted and hunted, and the Lombards were hunted down by the London mob. Then it was the turn of the French Protestants. I think that the same feelings holds good on this subject today. You always have a mob of uneducated people who will hunt down foreigners, and you always have people who will make use of the passions of this mob in order to get their own ends politically.[1]

The lingering effects of this traditional xenophobia are registered not only in the antipathy toward alien settlers of all kinds but also in the country's intense political and emotional responses to its residual colonial responsibilities in Zimbabwe, Kenya, Diego Garcia, and elsewhere. Britain's ambivalence about its empire is especially evident in its reactions to the fragments of brutal colonial history that emerge occasionally to unsettle the remembrance of the imperial project by undermining its moral legitimacy and damaging the national self-esteem. The terrifying folk knowledge of what is actually involved in being on the receiving end of imperial power has also been preserved and finds expression elsewhere—above all, in the country's intermittent fears of itself becoming a colonial dependency of the United States. This apprehension was expressed most vividly by Peter Kilfoyle, M.P., during the summer of 2003 when the disastrous character of the invasion of Iraq was becoming apparent. He pointed out that "the defence secretary Geoff Hoon, has acknowledged that we are to be to the US armed forces what the sepoys were to the British Indian Army."[2]

Each of the historical examples I have mentioned in passing can supply a detailed case study in support of my larger arguments. For example, the revelations about the brutal conduct of the war against "Mau Mau"

insurgents in Kenya that emerged on the fiftieth anniversary of the declaration of the eight-year "emergency" in that country warrant close attention in their own right, but they are also typical of the drip of embarrassing and uncomfortable information about imperial and colonial governance that has begun to leak into the public debate and challenge the
country's instinctive sense that its imperial ambitions were always good
and its political methods for realizing them, morally and legally defensi-
ble. This particular example involved allegations of brutality, torture, and
killing, which may compare favorably to the dismal record of other European powers elsewhere in Africa but nonetheless raised a host of issues
about the abuse of human rights and the characteristic manner in which
colonial wars were conducted. The shock involved in trying to accept that
British colonial administrators and soldiers, as well as the officials who
controlled them from Whitehall, could have been routinely involved in
such horrible practices did not exhaust the nation's feelings of discomfort
and shame at the conduct of its empire. Indeed, sticking with the Kenyan
case, those responses have been extended and amplified by various postcolonial conflicts. They have recently been compounded by another layer
of trauma that is directly relevant to the theme of this chapter. Though
their disturbing claims have been clouded by accusations of fraud,
Kenyan women from several generations have launched a legal action
against the British Ministry of Defence, which alleges that they were subjected to sexual assault by UK troops stationed in the area to conduct
"training exercises." Though the women involved were, unlike the insurgents of the earlier period, Masai rather than Kikuyu, these allegations
suggest governmental continuities between colonial and postcolonial
administrations that are united by a view of the natives as infrahuman
creatures to be preyed upon for sexual gratification. The women's controversial claims also included the additional charge that the British Army
had, over a thirty-year period, refused to investigate repeated allegations
of rape.

My argument is not principally concerned with the details involved in
these or various other similar legal actions, or indeed with the method-
ological and moral shifts that follow from approaching Britain's imperial
history through its victims' decisions to seek financial compensation for
their injuries by legal means. I am interested instead in the way that British
political culture has had to adapt in order to make sense of the catalogue
of horror that extends into the present from Morant Bay and Lucknow via
Londonderry and Dol Dol. I want us to consider the political and psychological reactions which attend the discovery that imperial administration
was, against all the ethnic mythology that projects empire as essentially a

form of sport, necessarily a violent, dirty, and immoral business. We need to know how that deeply disturbing realization has been managed and, in particular, to consider what consequences follow from the need to maintain the moral preeminence and progressive momentum that define colonial power as the redemptive extension of civilization into barbarity and chaos?

It is not only that the greatness of the British nation is evidently at still stake in the contested history of its difficult relationships with its colonial subjects. Repressed and buried knowledge of the cruelty and injustice that recur in diverse accounts of imperial administration can only be denied at a considerable moral and psychological cost. That knowledge creates a discomfiting complicity. Both are active in shaping the hostile responses to strangers and settlers and in constructing the intractable political problems that flow from understanding immigration as being akin to war and invasion. The hidden, shameful store of imperial horrors has been an unacknowledged presence in British political and cultural life during the second half of the twentieth century. It is not too dramatic to say that the quality of the country's multicultural future depends on what is now done with it. The history of empire directs attention to the practical mechanisms of racial hierarchy and the ideology of white supremacy, but that is not its only value to contemporary debates. Once those encounters have begun and a revised account of the nature of imperial statecraft has been folded into critical reflections on national life, the possibility of healing and reconciliation come into view. Sadly, the pressure of the past upon the present means that these difficulties are usually resolved in other, less-fruitful directions. The invitation to revise and reassess often triggers a chain of defensive argumentation that seeks firstly to minimize the extent of the empire, then to deny or justify its brutal character, and finally, to present the British themselves as the ultimate tragic victims of their extraordinary imperial successes. This outlook reaches its apogee in the work of Linda Colley, where it is combined with a great reluctance to see contemporary British racism as a product of imperial and colonial power. While I am with her when she stresses that "the British need to know much more about their impact in the past upon different regions of the world,"[3] we part company where the emphasis falls on the fact that Brits were passive "captives" of their imperial project and on the suggestion that their extensive global power was so multifaceted and locally complex that any generalizations about its uniformity, its racism, its ethics, and its military disposition must be postponed until it has been somehow fully understood. The desire to judge the empire harshly gets drowned in a swamp of squeamish equivocation.

Africans transported as slaves across the Atlantic experienced an atrocity that was not peculiar to the British empire, but was certainly fostered by it. In other contexts, however, the impact of empire was more uneven, sometimes very shallow and far more slow. Environments, economies, customs, power relations, and lives were sometimes devastated; but by no means always, because these intruders were frequently limited in number, and dependent often on a measure of indigenous tolerance.[4]

These telling words illuminate a larger cultural problem. They encapsulate what has become a widespread desire—to allocate a large measure of blame for the empire to its victims and then seek to usurp their honored place of suffering, winning many immediate political and psychological benefits in the process. Much of this embarrassing sentiment is today held captive by an unhealthy and destructive postimperial hungering for renewed greatness. Colley is again right in seeing that during the twentieth century, this desire feeds Britain's vicarious investments in U.S. preeminence. She is not, however, inclined to connect the desire for recovered greatness with the magical appeal of restored racial and ethnic homogeneity. The appeal of being great again was central to Mrs. Thatcher's premiership, particularly after her South Atlantic triumph, but it did not vanish with her. It has endured and mutated and emerged again as one significant element that propelled a largely reluctant country to war against Iraq in 2003. There was much more to this outcome than the New Labour info-warriors' desire to mimic the populist tempo of Thatcher's long and damaging political experiment. On the occasion of the anti-Saddam war, the geopolitical logic of Tony Blair's postideological oligarchy was running in a different direction from the spontaneous gestures of a not-yet-plural nation that desperately seemed to want to become something different, something less great but more noble, more consistent, and more autonomous.

Into The Streets

Mike Skinner of The Streets has explicitly voiced the alternative desire not to recover or repeat the conceits of empire but to shift into a different state of being in the world and "turn the page" of Britain's national history. In the year-long buildup to the outbreak of war, his poetic attempts to make the country more habitable by giving value to its ability to operate on a less-than-imperial scale were a notable counterpart to the totalizing ambitions of megapolitical government. Built upon the continuing aftershock of Rock Against Racism, which was a formative experience for the post-'68 generation, Skinner's songs share with Eliza Carthy's album *Anglicana* and Maggie Holland's Music Hall folk song "A Place Called England" a precious ability to transport English ethnicity into the present.[5] All of these interventions show that what Orwell would have regarded as an authentically geo-pious Anglo patriotism, can, in fact, be adapted to the demands of multicultural society. The singer Billy Bragg is another one of these awkward voices to have carried the debate over the cultural forms of the emergent, postimperial nation into the world of art-criticism. His rather worthy effort, "Take Down the Union Jack" redeems itself with his request for assent to the idea that "Gilbert and George are taking the piss." Certainly, the argument about postcolonial melancholia can place the nihilism of these and other, younger British artists in a very different setting. Unnoticed either by government or overground media culture, the emergent Britain for which Skinner's Streets supplied a witty and ambivalent mouthpiece mobilized traditional ideas of self-reliance and caution, insularity and fairness in order to make a range of bold, and in my view healthier claims about the condition of the country and the state of racial politics. These wittily delivered vernacular pronouncements were aimed toward the establishment of more modest and more explicitly democratic specifications of a revised national identity that is easier to appreciate and enjoy when it has removed itself from the world stage. This little England owes something to its nativist predecessors. It certainly shares their commitment to the relocalization of the world, but it has expanded their horizons and overcome their xenophobia. Racial difference is not feared. Exposure to it is not ethnic jeopardy but rather an unremarkable principle of metropolitan life. Race is essentially insignificant, at least when compared either to the hazards involved in urban survival or to the desperate pleasures of the postcolonial city: "sex and drugs and on the dole."

In The Streets' playful ontology, race is not an identity that can fix or contain individuals; it is a practice that can be understood through a comparison with the strategic choice of drug that a variety of person opts for in a particular situation: "whether you're white or black; smoke weed, chase brown, toot rock." More importantly, in this view of the nation the balance between its internal and external relations has been decisively adjusted. The imperial profile has become less appealing and, though the memory of war remains important, it is adapted to other purposes. The Streets' song "Turn the Page" suggests that the hope of a new national identity rests upon its reinterpretation. The song recasts the formative, traumatic memory of World War II as a rave. It is also compelling for the way that it refigures an English pastoral consciousness in an *urban* setting, breaking down the opposition between country and city and framing postcolonial Englishness with a recognizable trace of Orwell signaled by some casual ornithology:

> The sky turns white it all becomes clear
> they felt lifted from their fears
> they shed tears in the light after six dark years
> young bold soldiers the fire burns cracks and smoulders.
>
> . . . .
>
> the war is over, the bells ring
> memories fading, soldiers slaying
> looks like geezers raving
> the hazy fog over The Bullring
> the lazy ways the birds sing. . . . [6]

Skinner's fundamental concern with national collectivity is signaled by the song's shift from London to Birmingham. Along the way, the country has been actively reimagined as an ordered polity in a moral world of similar states capable of acting beyond self-interest in the spirit of cosmopolitan or, more accurately, planetary obligations that are opposed to the manifest injustices of globalization as Americanization: "round 'ere" he whines in a Brummie-Cockney hybrid accent, that emphatically asserts the priority of these local codes, "we say birds, not bitches."

The unexpected tide of popular opposition in 2003 to the British government's support for U.S. military power created opportunities to develop this revised conception of England and its adjusted role in the world. At that moment, it not only became possible to query the authoritarian versions of emancipatory modernization that had been served up in bad faith by New Labour but to imagine what it would be like to depart from the political and cultural templates of the nationalist mindset that Anthony Barnett identified long ago as "Churchillism." Churchill's name provided an especially appropriate term for this knot of imperial ideas and feelings because he had identified the uniqueness of Britain with its position at the junction of three distinct geopolitical formations: the north Atlantic world; the empire in its transition toward being a commonwealth; and Europe. This special location defined Britain's obligations and specified what had to be done in order to be and remain a great power. The rewards to the country would be substantial, especially if the disabling, socialistic habits of what we might now call "old Labour" could be disposed of. First, the Empire/Commonwealth and then the acquisition of nuclear weapons were critical in maintaining the stature of the country and in justifying its presence at the world's "top table." Postwar political administrations awarded different priorities to the various elements involved in managing this tripartite scheme, but its basic elements and their imagined relationship to the greatness that distinguishes Britain's character and genius have remained constant. Tony Blair's puzzling enthusiasm for gunboat diplomacy needs to be seen in this context. His resort to those old tactics registers the end of the political order in which the Soviet Union's global influence balanced American power and interests, but it is much better understood as the latest episode in a much longer and sorrier tale of the desperate things that British governments have done in order to mediate the worst effects of their inexorable decline. We should seize the chance to break with the Churchillist view of our nation and its interests before other campaigns, against Iran and Syria or even more simply against asylum seekers, who are the latest enemy within, drag us back in the same depressing direction once again. What follows is concerned with the cultural context and manifestations of this pathological formation and, of course, with the vibrant, ordinary multiculture that now opposes it.

Melancholia

The concept of melancholia essayed here and adapted to Britain's postcolonial conditions does not come into my arguments directly from its Freudian sources in discussions of narcissism, group psychology, and bereavement. It has arrived via the creative use made of those difficult insights in the pioneering social psychology of the German psychoanalysts Alexander and Margarete Mitscherlich. Their interpretation of social, psychological, and political behavior in postwar West Germany endeavored to understand the German people's melancholic reactions to the death of Hitler and to fathom the postwar demand that they face and work through the larger evil of which their love for him had been part. Faced with a sudden and radical loss of its moral legitimacy, the German nation warded off a collective process of mourning for what they had loved and lost by means of a depressed reaction that inhibited any capacity for responsible reconstructive practice.

The nation's accumulated guilt had been projected narrowly onto its fallen leader and his immediate accomplices. Bolstered by denial of the destructiveness and wickedness of Germany's war aims, that guilt intervened to block and defer the country's comprehension of its history. The ability to recall whole segments of the national past faded away, leaving destructive blank spaces in individual autobiographies and creating patterns of intergenerational complicity and conflict that contributed to a culture of alienation from and indifference not only to the past but "to anything that entails responsibility."[7]

The Mistcherlichs made a long, contentious, and complex argument, and I must inevitably oversimplify it here. They warn that melancholic reactions are prompted by "the loss of a fantasy of omnipotence" and suggest that the racial and national fantasies that imperial and colonial power required were, like those of the Aryan master race, predominantly narcissistic. From this perspective, before the British people can adjust to the horrors of their own modern history and start to build a new national identity from the debris of their broken narcissism, they will have to learn to appreciate the brutalities of colonial rule enacted in their name and to their benefit, to understand the damage it did to their political culture at home and abroad, and to consider the extent of their country's complex investments in the ethnic absolutism that has sustained it. The multilayered trauma—economic and cultural as well as political and psychological—involved in accepting the loss of the empire would therefore be compounded by a number of additional shocks. Among them are the painful obligations to work through the grim details of imperial and colonial history and to transform paralyzing guilt into a more productive shame that would be conducive to the building of a multicultural nationality that is no longer phobic about the prospect of exposure to either strangers or otherness.

This new phase of psychological and ethical maturity has emerged very slowly and unevenly among the political class. In marked contrast, the reflexive position outlined by The Streets and other similar voices has been unexpectedly close to the center of Britain's vernacular dissidence, lending energy to an ordinary, demotic multiculturalism that is not the outcome of governmental drift and institutional indifference but of concrete oppositional work: political, aesthetic, cultural, scholarly. This pressure from below has enriched and expanded the country's public sphere. I would like to bring about a new appreciation of this unheralded multiculture, which is distinguished by some notable demands for hospitality, conviviality, tolerance, justice, and mutual care.

Healthier patterns, in which Britain renounces its pursuit of greatness and reaps immediate benefits in civil society, are addressed to the very same historical moment and awareness that have solicited and even institutionalized the melancholic reaction I have been criticizing. The multiculturalism they articulate can usefully be identified with a mature response to diversity, plurality, and differentiation. It is oriented by routine, everyday exposure to difference. Postimperial melancholia, on the other hand, is associated with the neotraditional pathology of what, in the

British setting, Patrick Wright, who is its most acute observer, has identified as the morbidity of heritage.

I should emphasize that I do not see the larger mechanism at work here as something that is uniquely relevant to Britain. The modern histories of numerous other European countries, particularly Belgium, France, Spain, Italy, and the Netherlands, might also be used to construct equivalent arguments amidst the wreckage of their colonial extensions and the injustices of their inconsistent responses to immigration. These analyses would be based upon their obvious difficulties in acknowledging the pains and the gains that were involved in imperial adventures and upon the problems that have arisen from their inability to disentangle the disruptive results supposedly produced by an immigrant presence from the residual but potent effects of lingering but usually unspoken colonial relationships and imperial fantasies.

The historical experience of British world dominance and the accompanying habituation to imperial preeminence have no single iconic human cipher. Winston Churchill comes closer than Raleigh, Rhodes, Hawkins, or Nelson to being their imaginary embodiment, but perhaps because of the empire's extraordinary reach and duration, even his superhuman figure cannot stand in for it. The imperial domination with which his name has become synonymous generated an unprecedented condition of security and privilege. Today, those qualities have faded, but the imperial power that produced them is unmourned even when its potent residues intervene to make the restoration of British greatness imperative. The fragility of national life and the real value of empire would only be disclosed in the country's darkest and finest hours, from which Britain would be rescued by the sacrifice of its colonial soldiery.

Freud might have diagnosed this arrangement as an effect of the cultural urges that are capable of tipping whole civilizations or epochs into a neurotic state. In order to illuminate this "pathology of cultural communities" and to make sense of the way it has shaped the political fate of contemporary Britain, I want to propose that it is the infrahuman political body of the immigrant rather than the body of the sovereign that comes to represent all the discomforting ambiguities of the empire's painful and shameful but apparently nonetheless exhilarating history. The immigrant is now here because Britain, Europe, was once out there; that basic fact of global history is not usually deniable. And yet its grudging recognition provides a stimulus for forms of hostility rooted in the associated realization that today's unwanted settlers carry all the ambivalence of empire with them. They project it into the unhappy consciousness of their fearful and anxious hosts and neighbors. Indeed, the incomers may be unwanted and feared precisely because they are the unwitting bearers of the imperial and colonial past.

In this precarious national state, individual and group identifications converge not on the body of the leader or other iconic national object—Britannia recast in the guise of gym-trim Diana, the equally immortal Queen Mum, David Beckham's various haircuts, or even the beaming, sweaty figure of Prime Minister Blair himself—but in opposition to the intrusive presence of the incoming strangers who, trapped inside our perverse local logic of race, nation, and ethnic absolutism not only *represent* the vanished empire but also refer consciousness to the unacknowledged pain of its loss and the unsettling shame of its bloody management.

An important displacement mechanism becomes evident here. The arrival of these incomers, even when they were protected by their tenure of formal citizenship, was, as I have already said, understood to be an act of invasive warfare. That structure of feeling governs the continuing antipathy toward all would-be settlers. Later groups of immigrants may not, of course, be connected with the history of empire and colony in any way whatsoever. However, they experience the misfortune of being caught up in a pattern of hostility and conflict that belongs emphatically to its lingering aftermath. Once they recognize the salience of racial categories to their perilous predicament, it should not be surprising if these people try to follow the well-trodden path pioneered by the most vulnerable and marginal members of the host community. They too will seek salvation by trying to embrace and inflate the ebbing privileges of whiteness. That racialized identification is presumably the best way to prove they are not really immigrants at all but somehow already belong to the home-space in ways that the black and brown people against whom they have to compete in the labor market will never be recognized as doing.

As is well known, Enoch Powell's notorious speeches on immigration played with these powerful feelings of aggression, guilt, and fear and articulated them as a violent racist politics. We should think back to his memorable imagery not of the "rivers of blood," which in 1968 he predicted would be the catastrophic outcome of all Britain's mistaken attempts to mix the races, but of the even more terrifying prospect of a wholesale reversal of the proper ordering of colonial power. A plain-speaking, Brummie informant provided the point of departure for Powell's whole argument with a racist warning that "in this country in fifteen or twenty years time the black man will have the whip hand over the white man."[8] That awful prospect was intended to be scary. It has subsequently provided the justification for many a preemptive strike like the one that took Stephen Lawrence's life in 1993.

In practice, the colonial strangers' disturbingly intimate association with their mother country was always qualified by the exclusionary workings of informal institutions like the "Colour Bar." Nevertheless, the citizen-settlers appeared confident that their reasonable requests for hospitality would eventually be heard and understood. They had no idea that those demands were impossible to fulfill within the fantastic structures of the melancholic island race. The requests for fairness only increased the problems because the inevitable refusals precipitated a further cycle of violence and guilt. This was itself intensified by feelings of resentment, rejection, and fear at the prospect of open interaction with an otherness, which could only be imagined as loss and jeopardy.

Britain's inability to mourn its loss of empire and accommodate the empire's consequences developed slowly. Its unfolding revealed an extensively fragmented national collective that has not so far been able to meet the elemental challenge represented by the social, cultural, and political transition with which the presence of postcolonial and other sanctuary-seeking people has been unwittingly bound up. Instead, racist violence provides an easy means to "purify" and rehomogenize the nation. As one might anticipate, postimperial and postcolonial melancholia characteristically intercut this violence and the shame-faced tides of self-scrutiny and self-loathing that follow among decent folk, with outbursts of manic euphoria.

The widespread influence of this odd combination of responses can be illustrated by a range of cultural and political phenomena. Its imprint has been consistently evident in various official and semiofficial statements on race and immigration. The Home Secretary David Blunkett has, for example, made a number of irreconcilable policy statements in this area that can usefully be interpreted in this light. Blunkett righteously denounced the *Sun* newspaper as racist and attacked the BBC as "Powellite" for the sensationalist way that it played up the dangers that asylum seekers represent and emphasized the governments' failure to manage their presence. However, his righteous indignation did not extend to any self-criticism. Blunkett seemed to have forgotten that he had been inclined to do exactly the same thing himself, that he had revived Enoch Powell's discourse of "repatriation" and announced in a populist tone borrowed from the Murdoch press that Britain's asylum seekers should "get back home and rebuild their own countries."[9] Anthony Giddens, the distinguished social scientist and a close associate of the government, suggested that a Blairite "Third Way" in this difficult field of social policy could be identified through the contradictory policy objectives involved in simultaneously being "tough on immigration, but tough on the causes of hostility to immigrants."[10] Any promise in this bewildering proposal was undone by the obvious fact that hostility to popular immigrants was being fostered by the mainstream politicians who were then to be charged with the mission of being tough on themselves! They are apparently fearful of being outflanked on the right by xenophobia and ultranationalism but reluctant to concede their complicity with the way that anti-immigrant feeling dominates the political debate.

Racist and nationalist responses that were pioneered by populist opposition to commonwealth immigration during the 1950s and 1960s remain the backbone of this resistance to convivial culture. The same kind of symptomatic contradiction can even be noted in the conclusions to Sir William Macpherson's celebrated report of inquiry into the murder of Stephen Lawrence, the official document that marked the latest event in the fitful emergence of the country's racial conscience. Macpherson's epoch-making report anchored the most recent phase of reforms and helped to bring anti-racist goals closer to the governmental process. His well-publicized adjustments to the concept of institutional racism have become legendary, but they are also marked by postcolonial melancholia. Though the good judge acknowledged that prejudice was indeed present in Britain's system of criminal justice, he then emphasized the idea that this dysfunctional racism was "unwitting." He was saying, in effect, that racism's perpetrators should not be seen as wholly responsible for the outcome of their actions. To be sure, he identified institutional racism with collective organizational failures of British legal and governmental agencies, but he then provided a definition of what counted as racist that was so narrowly and tightly drawn that it excluded almost everybody and left the sources of these persistent but mysterious failures inaccessible to all but the most sophisticated management consultants.[11] Similar oscillations can be detected in other pronouncements and policies. Indeed, those characteristic oscillations are audible wherever race and absolute ethnicity have been made intelligible as matters of law and government.

Another avowedly liberal social commentator, Paul Barker, responded to the murderous shooting of four black girls at a Birmingham party with a *Guardian* article that was notable for its refusal to concede that the grandchildren of the postwar citizen-immigrants could actually be substantively British. Barker went so far as to argue that their record of violent crimes added up to putting the entire civilizing process "into reverse." He offered a narrow, ethnic definition of the killings, seeing them as a result of a specifically Jamaican predisposition to the fashion of gun crime. Proposing more ruthless and aggressive policing as the only appropriate response to this worrying development, he outlined a negative view not of black criminals but of the very idea of black community. His words revived the ungenerous opinions of the right-wing commentators who had responded to the impact of Macpherson's report by saying that its remedies were disproportionate to the extent of the country's problems because Britain had no substantive or coherent black community. "It's hard to know in what sense Caribbeans in Britain are a community," Barker opined. "For some years they embodied what immigration meant. . . . The Caribbean community seems to be disintegrating, or is being abandoned. The marrying out (or partnering out) rates are extraordinary. As older people retire, many return to the Caribbean."[12] The absence of recognizable community supplies a justification for more robust police tactics, which are, in turn, explained by Barker's resort to what he calls a "Benthamite" approach to the rights of minorities. The greatest good of the greatest number was his benchmark against which the character and the outcome of new police initiatives was to be considered. Barker made much of the fact that Macpherson's report had not condemned the deployment of "stop and search" tactics by the police, even though these approaches have been associated with racial discrimination, police harassment, and injustice over long periods of time. In Barker's case, his evident relish at the prospect of finally doing something about burgeoning black crime was linked not only to understandable depression and disgust at its effects but also to a barely suppressed sense of discomfort at the distance from official liberalism that racial politics had induced him to travel. There seemed to be a measure of self-disgust and a different form of depression at stake in his presentation of these horrible killings as an exemplary moment in which liberals like himself had to draw a deep breath, grit their teeth, and, in the face of baffling black savagery, renounce their liberalism.

These patterns have been swirling around in debates over black criminality for decades. Many of the continuing responses to Macpherson's report reveal similar aspects or suggest melancholia's signature combination of manic elation with misery, self-loathing, and ambivalence. Hostility to the proposition that racist violence and institutional indifference are normal and recurrent features of British social and political life gets intermingled with absolute and sincere surprise at the nastiness of racism and the extent of the anger and resentment that it can cause. Antipathy toward asylum seekers and refugees cannot be concealed, but the idea that it has anything to do with racism or ultranationalism remains shocking and induces yet more guilt. This confusion and disorientation result from a situation in which melancholic Britain can concede that it does not like blacks and wants to get rid of them but then becomes uncomfortable because it does not like the things it learns about itself when it gives vent to feelings of hostility and hatred.

The other end of this chain of meaning has for the last few years lain in anxiety over the fate of Britain's abandoned colonial kith and kin in the Falklands, in Africa, and particularly in Robert Mugabe's Zimbabwe. This too is a long story. The repetition of tragic southern African themes—the interminable saga of Julie Ward's murder, the massive coverage for sexual and other violent assaults on holiday makers and tourists[13]—are a notable feature of this moment not only because they convey the catastrophic consequences of intermixture and the severe problems that arise once colonial order has been withdrawn or sacrificed but because, like Linda Colley's recent work and Enoch Powell's "rivers of blood" speech, they are deployed to contest and then seize the position of victim. Taking possession of that coveted role can also be linked to a sustained academic attempt to rehabilitate the imperial idea and enhance colonial history so that it can play a proper role in the redefinition of national sovereignty, a move required by the military humanism of the gunboat diplomats who, in the words of Tony Blair's adviser, the diplomat Robert Cooper, promote the application of "double standards." There is now one law for the "postmodern" West, another for the chaotic world of failed, incompetent, and premodern states. For Cooper, these operations now involve a self-conscious reversion to "the rougher methods of an earlier era—force, preemptive attack, deception, whatever is necessary to deal with those who still live in the nineteenth-century world of every state for itself."[14]

The very ease with which the ideologues of this strategy reach for the concept of empire as a benign and dynamic guarantor of progress betrays how much ground they still have to cover if they are ever to work through its history and, once melancholia has been succeeded by mourning, start to produce a new image of the nation that can accommodate its colonial dimensions. Again, this is not just a British problem. In France, the publication of General Paul Aussaresses' popular memoir of the war in Algeria, with its unrepentant defense of torture as practical political technique, has created a recognizable pattern of equivocation, denial, and mock horror.[15] It bears repetition that retelling these colonial stories projects the imperial nation as the primary victim rather than the principal beneficiary of its vanished colonial dominance. This variety of discourse is also common to the populist politicians who now profess an inability even to recognize our country since the arrival of postcolonial aliens has decisively altered its moral and cultural topography. I should emphasize that these problems precede and underpin the poetics of *racial*, *national*, and ethnic difference that makes them comprehensible. I must also insist that the country's persistent failure to be hospitable is about far more than just managing the internal effects of mass immigration. It cannot be said too often that this is not, at source, a matter of "race," even though, for many people, it is understood and lived as such. It is the workings of racism that produce the order of racial truths and not the other way around.

The consolidation of postcolonial melancholia suggests an even more disturbing possibility, namely that many people in Britain have actually come to need "race" and perhaps to welcome its certainties as one sure way to keep their bearings in a world they experience as increasingly confusing. For them, there can be no working through this problem because the melancholic pattern has become the mechanism that sustains the unstable edifice of increasingly brittle and empty national identity. The nation's intermittent racial tragedies become part of an eventful history. They punctuate the boredom of chronic national decline with a functional anguish. The loss of empire—and the additional loss of certainty about the limits of national and racial identity that result from it—have begun, ironically, to sustain people, providing them with both pleasure and distraction. The historical approach tentatively pioneered here tries to seek out a less regular narrative rhythm than strict, even oscillation between identification with the victims of racism, a guilty dislike of them and the changes they have made to the country, and tormented self-disgust at the prospect of being implicated either in the problems they import or in their colonial and postcolonial sufferings.

Two World Wars and One World Cup

Here I must pause over Britain's odd culture of sports *spectatorship* and its relationship to xenophobia, racism, and war. This formation is connected to but is far from identical with the culture of sport that was mapped onto the country's cultures of war and empire for a very long time. The political language of sport remains important today. It has become a pivotal element in the elaboration of the New Labour populism, which tried to cash in on football and then manipulate enthusiasm for the idea that the country could stage the World Cup or the Olympic Games.[16] It matters also because it is around sport that more habitable and, I am tempted to say, more modern formations of national identity have been powerfully articulated. On the most basic level, the signature of this shift has been the substitution of the more pliable associations of the flag of St. George for those of the discredited Union Jack. This should not be understood as another tidy binary. The blurring of boundaries between England

and Britain on which this shift has relied is itself part of the opportunity that I sense in this phase of cultural and political transition.

For about three decades, the brash motto of true-Brit sporting nationalism was supplied by a curious boast: "Two world wars and one World Cup, doo dah, doo dah." Future historians will doubtless puzzle over this odd phrase, which, as it echoed around many British sports venues, became an ugly chant. They will probably struggle to make sense of the strange symbolic system in which the words circulated and grasp the warped patriotism to which they gave disturbing expression. The visceral ideas and feelings that these words conjured up have an enduring appeal, but they have slipped past most academic analyses of popular nationalist politics. For the most part, the full, historic force of this fraternalistic and class-bound braggadocio has not been registered in the beleaguered places where the history of Britain's sporting cultures and the political analysis of its popular nationalism are still being invented.

Those chanted words should not be passed over because they appear initially to be mindless or insignificant. The intellectual commitment to taking these sentiments seriously, to making them worth understanding and unpacking, involves recognizing the dignity and value of the worthy lives that motto has helped to lead astray or divert into the arid lands of Brit nationalist fantasy. For anyone willing to dig a little past the bright surface of its red, white, and blue crust, that phrase will supply a wealth of valuable insights into the morbid culture of a once-imperial nation that has not been able to accept its inevitable loss of prestige in a determinedly postcolonial world. Rather like that other epochal phrase, "There Ain't No Black in the Union Jack," which served a similar function in various British sports grounds for a while, the explicit linkage of war to football provides a rare window from which all the remorseful processes of Britain's vanished imperial status can be observed. In this light, the phrase "two world wars and one World Cup" becomes a means through which to consider the bewildering effects of England's postcolonial melancholia—even where they have been intermittently offset by the compensations of the country's rare but nonetheless significant sporting successes. The phrase furnishes us with a compressed but still priceless history of postwar class relations in what is harder these days to call the United Kingdom. All the latent violence, all the embittered machismo, all the introjected class warfare articulated by defeated victors (mostly men and boys who were baffled and bewildered by a new postwar world that refused to recognize their historic manly qualities) is coded here in a dynamic and still explosive form.

Those words and sounds—"two world wars and one World Cup, doo dah, doo dah"—suggest firstly, and most disturbingly, that war is a type of sport. Secondly, they introduce the possibility that sport, particularly football, has the same value as war in the circuits of our distinctive national economy. This twist is a local "postcolonial" peculiarity of English life, and it demands detailed historical consideration. It is not just that the two fields—war and sport—are adjacent in the metonymic chain of Britain's reluctantly postimperial nationalisms. We are also being told that they should be understood as intimately connected areas of the country's national consciousness. Once they have been rendered equivalent and perhaps even interchangeable, we can see that war and sport generate many of the same emotions. They articulate the same libidinal investments and mobilize the same intense and highly prized forms of fraternal solidarity. The surrogate wars that were previously enacted only on the playing field become a better, more exciting game when they are extended after the sporting formalities have been dispensed with. Opposing fans, foreign police, and any local "aliens" unlucky enough to get in the way have all contributed to the body count on these nation-building excursions. This absurd phrase contains a deeply and spontaneously conservative assertion of national continuity. It expresses not national history but an antihistory governed by the familiar amnesiac principles by which deluded nations live. Whether and how the world these words create is to be racialized is still being negotiated and depends on more than the durability of Arsenal's black cosmopolis. The boast to which the phrase gives voice is integral to a larger denial. It declares that nothing significant changed during the course of Britain's downwardly mobile twentieth century. Under a tattered flag, the precious thin red, white, and blue line remains unbreached, just like the crumbling, chalky frontier down at Dover where Mathew Arnold felt the earth move beneath his feet. We are being required to admit that the nations which triumphed in 1918 and 1945 live on somewhere unseen, but palpable. They are essentially unmodified and their continuity is, for the most part, unremarked upon. An implicit challenge invites us to discover their untimely, contentious definitions of homogenous nationality again today as a lingering, gritty presence inside the glittery but battered package of Britain's perennially suspended modernization.

The same phrase, "two world wars and one World Cup," testifies backhandedly to the continuing power of class-based political language. In a stroke, it repudiates the fashionable notion that casual and informal status hierarchies have now replaced the destructive architecture of an obviously class-divided nation with a more appealing new arrangement, in which class and regional divisions are more evenly blended or perhaps altogether dispersed. Phony King Tony and his crony courtiers may cynically dream of making populist politics out of lowering the exorbitant price of replica football kits. He may even appear from time to time in his best referee's shorts and profess his undying support for Newcastle United, but no matter where his own constituency is located, he is nowhere near to being a Geordie. Indeed, his brazen, utterly implausible claim to belong to the political body of that slumbering colossus, has, like Paul Gascoigne's tragic boozy antics, thrown the shifting dynamics of what we should probably call Geordie "ethnicity" into sharp relief.

It would seem that postindustrial Britain's class divisions adhere stubbornly to the regional and geopolitical patterns of its ebbing industrial phase. They are clearly alive and well. Inequality is being intensified and re-created; sport and its various spectator cultures are producing, reproducing, and channeling nationalist and absolutist identifications and identities. They appear in acute and attractive forms that must now compete with the rootless cosmopolitanism of mercenary players drawn from every corner of the world who are then required to represent and enact its localization in the match-day ritual.

The chanted phrase has a perlocutionary power. This atavistic force is little understood, but it can effectively *produce* the artificially whitened, comprehensively rehomogenized national community to which ultranationalist discourse casually refers. The fleeting appearance of this community can also demonstrate that there are still many courageous and willing working-class hearts beating around here. The martial—I am forced to say, Churchillian—performances in which those magic words, "two world wars and one World Cup," are incanted communicate another significant hint about the character of the nation that is being assembled. Those words reveal that there is a sense in which Britain's brave but confused affiliates prefer an ordered past in which they were exploited and pauperized, but nonetheless knew who they were, to a chronically chaotic present in which even those limited certainties have been stripped away by the new corporate mandate of interminable, regressive change. In the nation's mud-and-blood-spattered past, heroic lions were led to ignominious slaughter by posh donkeys. Today, at last, their belated but incomplete redemption is finally at hand. It is to be accomplished not so much by any occasional national victories on the sports field but by another characteristic national accomplishment: an unblinking and unthinking pride in sporting performances that is indifferent as to whether the worthy lions in question are ultimately victorious.

The Gentlemen have died out or moved on to more consistently remunerative pastures. They have abandoned the sports field, leaving it in the well-paid but horny hands of The Players. As the aristocrats flee from team games and reconstitute their community with the aid of horses and hounds, we are confronted by one worthwhile international competition in which true Brits will not be bested by wily, elegant, wine-drinking eye-ties and girly, shampoo-selling frogs or shamed by the overdisciplined ranks of mechanical, unfeeling krauts who don't know the *volkish* meanings of a warm pint let alone the traditional joys of a kebab or a chicken tikka, never mind an extra bag of chips. England's traditional foolhardiness, pluck, and "up and at 'em" daring combine with a monstrously exaggerated sense of the country's importance to ensure that Brits will triumph in the national pride stakes every time. This triumphant conquest entails a more profound and total victory than any merely sporting contest can be made to contain.

The phrase "two world wars and one World Cup" reveals its more melancholy and sinister aspects once the adrenalin begins to subside. It is deployed (but inevitably fails) to block consciousness of the irreversible fact that the carnival of Britain's imperial potency is now over forever. Any residual celebrations to which the words contribute help to constitute not the final stages of that stirring jubilee but the protracted process of cleaning up that follows it. This chant supplies an appropriate vernacular soundtrack to the mournful task of taking down the bunting. The party is certainly over, but "two world wars and one World Cup" can be articulated as an overdue invitation as well as a battle cry. Come and celebrate, it says, come to the national necropolis. Come and drink and shout and fight. Johnny foreigner needs a lesson in patriotism and we will be handing it out—doo dah doo dah. We may not win many games but we do know how to support our side—doo dah doo dah.

The historical record of England's belligerent fans "on tour" is dismal and well known. But there is still a great deal of reluctance to identify these recurrent and depressing symptoms as part of the country's wider topography of ultranationalist or racial consciousness. It should be understood that this refusal compounds all the injuries involved in racial exclusion and ethnic absolutism. Those of us who have had to run for our lives from vicious drunken crowds intent on a different, bloodier sport than the one they paid to see on the terraces have always been able to know where nationalist sentiments were wired in to the raciological circuitry of the British nation and where Brit racisms and nationalisms were fused together as something like a single ethnic gestalt.

This easy intermingling is not just an issue for English fans. The same fears and conceits have a wider resonance in the nationalist aspirations of the United Kingdom's minor nations. Even when defined explicitly against imperial England, their dreams of nationality have been enhanced by ideals of purity and fantasies of homogeneity. The knot of ideas around sport demonstrates that we cannot sanction the luxury of believing that "race," nation, and ethnicity will be readily or easily disentangled from each other. Brit nationalism cannot be purged of its racialized contents any more easily than a body can be purged of the skeleton that supports it. Doubtless, the full implications of that realization will one day transform the conduct of British political life. Let us hope that many more people will not have to die before the penny finally drops. In the meantime, there is more proof that English nationalism remains volatile material. Manipulative politicians should not play with it, even if they have persuaded themselves that they can harness its populist magic to benign and wholesome ends. Wherever nationalism is politically engaged, all the violent perversity of race thinking will not be far away.

Football is itself changing as national and local leagues decline as part of a wider transition toward supranational audiences and global branding. Though, as we have seen, absolute nationalism is reactively expressed in that space, we must thank the commercial acumen of Alan Sugar, Ken Bates, and Rupert Murdoch for the fact that an emergent cosmopolitanism is now, tentatively, evident there too. Real-time encounters in the stadium are increasingly becoming the preserve of the wealthy, while the television transmissions are monopolized by Murdoch's empire. Under these unprecedented conditions, it is by no means clear which cultural tendency will eventually triumph. It may take the formation of a pan-European super league to consolidate a new set of regional ties and translocal loyalties that could make the option of absolute ethnicity less attractive than it appears to be at present. Pending that outcome, different patterns of marketing and visibility are evident in other sports and spectacles. The same historic chemistry of "race," ethnicity, and national belonging has certainly touched them too, but the effects have not always been destructive. Men's cricket is in what appears to be a serious decline as a national spectator sport. Its old imperial logics are lost, and its civilizing codes are increasingly anachronistic and unmoving in a world sharply and permanently divided into the two great camps—a select group of winners and an ever-expanding legion of losers whose plight is more acutely represented by the TV-friendly tempo of basketball than the languor of cricket. Few state schools have the time or the facilities to maintain teams. Tall children want to play basketball rather than bowl, and the fundamental idea that a wholly satisfying contest can endure for five days and yet produce no result increasingly defies comprehension. Meanwhile, the dead weight of a corrosive class culture and regional differences within the country prevent the decomposing game from reinventing itself.

A distinctive pattern of sporting events has accented the rhythm of Britain's racialized politics during the second half of the twentieth century. These episodes—including the watershed World Cup victory of 1966, the "blackwash" cricket series against the all-conquering West Indies during the 1970s, Virginia Wade's jubilee-year win at Wimbledon, Diego Maradona's "hand of God" goal, the tearful exit from Italia 90, the riots of Euro 96, the deaths at Heysel and Hillsborough, and the football team's amazing successes in the Japanese World Cup of 2002—might productively be seen as staging posts en route to a more complex sense of Englishness and English culture in which greatness is tempered by the process of living with feelings of defeat. The same historical sequence invites us to ask what the fame of Daley Thompson, Frank Bruno, and Linford Christie—and the more ephemeral celebrity of Denise Lewis, Sonia Lannaman, Fatima Whitbread, Tessa Sanderson, Zola Budd, Vinnie Jones, and many, many long-forgotten others—tell us about the nation that we live in. By revealing the nation's heroes and manifesting its more fantastic desires, this patriotic pantheon asks us systematically to reconsider the significance of the misty evening on which Viv Anderson made his international debut as the first black player to pull on an England shirt.

Of course, overt, respectable politics seldom intrudes into the avowedly un- and emphatically antipolitical sports mediascape, which is apparently populated by graying and balding ghosts and other, more tragic alcoholic shadows of long-vanished greatness. Deprived of a political compass to orientate us, we are required to explore the strange meaning of John Barnes' appearance on an overcrowded platform supporting Margaret Thatcher's Conservative Party and to understand how the authoritarian inclinations revealed in his autobiography could combine with his great dignity and exemplary sensitivity in comforting the relatives of ordinary Scouse people whose lives had been squandered by sniggering police at Hillsborough. Away from Merseyside, where "You'll Never Walk Alone" would always eclipse the strains of "Abide With Me," never mind the pieties of "God Save the Queen," Barnes was never a hero. Jimmie Greaves and company made his exclusion from the inner circle of British sporting greatness a matter of national honor. Barnes' private education had also made him a marked man, but he could never really be one of them/us while he retained a Jamaican passport. All the historic perfidies of the postwar race-relations industry were laid on his shoulders and then made incarnate in the dazzling image of that Afro-haired traitor in a white shirt streaking past all those gobsmacked Brazilian defenders in the Maracana stadium. A cat can be born in a kipper box, but that, as we've been sagely told in a cynical echo of neo-Fascist discourse, will never make it into a kipper. His successors have had to adopt different tactics that, where they have been successful—and I have the long and belligerent career of Paul Ince in mind—have had the additional virtue of underlining the insubstantiality of racial difference when compared to the power of class, masculinity, and stupidity.

All these sorry tales might be orchestrated so as to culminate in the controversial visits of Mike Tyson to Britain's wretched inner cities or, more accurately, in Tyson's moving response to news of Frank Bruno's breakdown and hospitalization.[17] Tyson's rapturous reception by many of Britain's poor and marginal men, both black and white, was also noted by The Streets in their acutely observed and chilling exploration of the everyday symptoms of the country's relentless meltdown, "Has It Come to This?" Tyson's continuing popularity suggests that there is plenty of life left in the patterns of identification, desire, and connection originally established early in the century by sporting figures whose unassailable heroism first defined the era of mass culture and showed the way toward the globalization of sporting spectacle. Appreciating the novelty of this pattern and its links to new kinds of commerce and capital also requires that we grasp another discomforting possibility. It is not primarily class that is at stake in these connections but the translocal integrity both of the male body and the appeal of the idea of manliness, which has become such an ambiguous and contested factor in the cultural economy of "race" and nation. Here, perhaps, are the deepest latent meanings of the national family romance, of poor, falsetto Becks dressed up in Posh's expensive underwear or with his dyed hair plaited into corn rows shaking hands with Nelson Mandela. The lost key to all those puzzling layers of sentimentality that have recently saturated the political landscape can now be discovered hidden in Linford's lunchbox. Once again, spectator sport is the fitting cipher in which these historic confrontations are knowingly transmitted and unknowingly received. Understanding the centrality of race to this cultural shift and the political forms with which it is intertwined creates an opportunity for revaluing sport and its cultures. We can begin to appreciate them not for their contribution to the country's melancholia, but for the fleeting, prefigurative glimpses of a different nation that they have unwittingly provided.

The Cultural Complex of Postcolonial Melancholia

The cultural disorientation that accompanies the collapse of imperial certainties into postcolonial nihilism has also been answered in other ways.

One of its features has been a publishing bonanza dominated by books that either seek to diagnose or remedy the national pathology. This is a huge phenomenon that can only be represented sketchily here by weighty tomes from some distinguished diagnosticians of the nation's predicament. Among them are Jeremy Paxman's best-selling work *The English*, described by Henry Porter on the back in the following terms, which are both glowing and revealing: "As good and as funny a description of the current state of our race as you will find anywhere."[18] Peter Ackroyd's voluminous *Albion* is also part of this trend.[19] He offers a historical survey of the proceedings of the English imagination that is also memorable for its casual employment of the language of race in order to articulate the English particularity—"a sense of longing and belonging"—that he finds lodged in the mutual embrace of "reverence for the past" and "affinity with the natural landscape."

An Elegy For England is a slimmer, more serious autobiographical volume from the Conservative wit and philosopher Roger Scruton.[20] His volume shares their geo-piety, though he is prepared to be more explicit than the others about the nature of England's present difficulties and the chronic problems in its political culture that reproduce them. He agrees with the other two in showing how English culture, at least until it was wrecked by "dumbing down," was consistently enriched by the contributions made to it by immigrants. He describes how that productive arrangement broke down under the pressure of extending citizenship to twentieth-century commonwealth migrants "from the former empire who seized on the idea of British nationality as a means of having no real nationality at all, certainly no nationality that would conflict with ethnic or religious loyalties, forged far away and years before."[21] Once again, when race becomes an issue a melancholic tone becomes audible. He continues, "the disquiet over immigration was the result . . . not of racism, but of the disruption of an old experience of home, and a loss of enchantment which made home a place of safety and consolation." The obvious reply to this mournful observation would be to point out that making postcolonial immigrants appear to be exclusively responsible for that "disruption" was Enoch Powell's notable contribution to postwar British political culture. In the world beyond Enoch's peculiar personal nightmares of bloody racial war, that disruption of home was not produced by the efforts of postcolonial settlers. Their own search for living room and their naïve expectation of hospitality did, however, coincide with it. Since that fatal moment, various fantasies of their expulsion have furnished the cheapest and most straightforward means to hold fear, anxiety, and sadness over the loss of empire at bay. At that point, these vulnerable but hopeful people became, as Stuart Hall had pointed out in 1974, central to British society's "quarrel with itself."[22] In fact, the process that Scruton identifies as a loss of home is, as he himself seems to sense, the result of a huge range of factors for which immigrants cannot reasonably be held responsible: economic decline, the impact of privatization and consumerism, the steady debasement of political culture, the evacuation of hope and meaning from everyday life, the erosion of family and household intimacy, and the increasing poverty of communicable experience are just a few that spring immediately to mind. The question remains: Why should these anxieties have fastened onto to race and immigration as the primary cause of the nation's woes, or, to put it another way, why do they generate racism and nationalism as the primary responses to problems that strangers and aliens import. And then, why do they promote the magical rehomogenization of the country as the favored solution to its postcolonial plight? Yet another predictable round of melancholic anguish ensues at the point where it is discovered that English kids call 911 rather than 999 when they want the help of the police, that they are now eating too much fast food and becoming obese at U.S. rates or that their traditional vowels are being Australianized.

The consensus of these esteemed authors seems to be that a special combination of reverence for the past and the unique English affinity for what Ackroyd bizarrely calls the "natural" landscape will guarantee an inexhaustible current of ethnically characteristic imaginative cultural work. An infusion of appropriate forms of culture and their incorporation into revised school curricula will slow down or even repair the damage that has already been done. It is telling that the power of the landscape emerges as the dominant element here. This outcome is troubling because it excludes all urban and metropolitan spaces from the forms of moral and aesthetic rearmament that are necessary if the country is to be reinvigorated and restored. However, this is not the timeworn Churchillian response which casts its eyes outward in pursuit of the healing power of greatness. This operation turns inward, seeking resources for national renewal in the treasure trove of Englishness. It can still be located if the right sort of maps are employed. Their topography can be deduced from all the obvious traditional sources—crown, church, and the countryside—but all of them are currently tainted, respectively by divorce and family breakdown, by the acceptance of homosexual clergy, and by the crisis of farming and the marketing of frankenfoods. The malign influence of Princess Diana upon the traditional authority of the crown is still being registered in postcolonial revelations such as her son's twenty-first birthday party's having an "out-of-Africa" theme. In May 2003, the *Sun* revealed with a shudder that "Rooms at Windsor Castle would be transformed into the African Bush, with food and drink matching the mood of the night . . . the invitations feature a charging elephant." Sadly, more details were not forthcoming.

Different, pure, and unimpeachable alternatives to all this have to be found. The sterling image of the nation that derives from its mythology of righteous anti-Nazi war—victimage, unimpeachable moral authority, and then eventual triumph—is prominent among them. This is the point at which the comforting rumble of Spitfires and Hurricanes can be heard approaching in the distance.

Orwell's vital legacy of disenchanted and anti-imperial cosmopolitics suffers greatly in these circumstances. His credibility as a patriotic celebrant of English nature is high, his mastery of the language unmatched—at least in his essays—and, if some of his wilder political opinions are likely to raise eyebrows, they can always be excused as juvenilia. His political record is checkered enough to invite him to be made over as a man of the Right who retained all the conservative instincts of the class from which he had originally fled. Precisely this dumbed-down version of Orwell was, for example, cited at the time by Home Secretary Jack Straw as part of the Blair government's ill-starred attempts to reclaim patriotism for the Left and presumably to distinguish its valuable positive, populist, and anti-immigrant qualities from the nationalism of groups like the BNP. For Straw, it was the Left's refusal to be patriotic that had brought about the hijacking of modern British identity by conservative forces and awarded a political monopoly of these potent populist themes to the Right. Though Straw drew heavily on his authority, Orwell had described the distinction between patriotism and nationalism in altogether different terms. He defined nationalism expansively as "the habit of assuming that human beings can be classified like insects and that whole blocks of millions or tens of millions of people can be confidently labelled good or bad."[23] Not long after, Orwell's centenary provided the setting for a further frightening development we might call the "which Blair project." It saw his complex legacy pulled hither and thither by conservative and radical opinions, both of which were desperate to monopolize it in furtherance of their particular agendas. Orwell's principled decision to fight in Spain can be twisted into a humanitarian act akin to the cosmopolitan liberation of Iraq or Afghanistan.

We are returned time and again to the instrumentalization and trivialization of war, which are primary symptoms of this whole cultural complex. That recurrence directs attention not only toward the figure of the reluctant citizen-soldier but also to the test of British maleness that the new war against immigrants and aliens involves. It becomes important to consider the anxious masculinity that has been celebrated in the hugely popular novels of writers like Tony Parsons and Nick Hornby. There are many differences between them, but there is also much that they share: their focus on masculinity, their contempt for Feminism, and their quiet but steady advocacy of the wholesale privatization of both experience and government. The tension between public and private values supplied the central theme of Hornby's *How to Be Good*, an amusing novel that articulates his political outlook in a conclusion where the backdrop to responsible domesticity and parenting, its condition of possibility, is the effective disappearance of the world beyond the confines of home and family.[24] The Thatcherite retooling of the nation—"there is no such thing as society, there are men, there are women, there are families"—was tidily transposed into New Labour common sense.

Parsons' lowbrow efforts project characters whose masculinity conforms to the pattern described in the author's well-publicized opinion that the political and cultural generation to which he and Blair belong (not to mention Paxman, Ackroyd, and Scruton) is somehow not authentically male because it has never been tested in battle. He calls them "the fuck around fuck up and fuck off generation." Speaking of his own relationship to Harry Silver, the protagonist of his most successful pieces, *Man and Boy* and *Man and Wife*, Parsons put it like this: "What I share with Harry is a love of family, respect for parents and an adoration of children. But he's different from me. He's much nicer; more agonised about his failings and lapses. I'm much more of a ruthless bastard. Is he a real man? In my heart, I don't think you're a real man if you haven't fought in a war." Parsons' literary world is scarcely more complicated than this declaration, and I think it accounts for the great appeal of his books. Harry covets his father's war service in the commandos, his single-minded discipline, his certainty, and the tacit power that is lodged in his domestic hierarchy, even if it is unmatched by anything that befalls him outside the home. These qualities derive from the pre-Feminist world that formed him. They are the core of the books, though, to be fair, Parsons also wants to show appreciation for the all-around competence and irrepressible spirit of hard-boiled women like his mother, members of the last generation to make their own clothes. Their toughness is a result not of their poverty, their class, or their marriages but of the stability that derives from their contented place in a firmly and appropriately gendered world. The authentic measure of Parsons' post-Feminist protagonist does not lie in his being able to heal himself and become a better man through intimate contact with his son. We are supposed to believe that he loves the boy too much for that strategy to be tried out. Harry's redemption derives instead from the fact that he can usurp the place of the child's mother, whose failures in her role as a wife have been obscured by a shallow critique of his infidelity.

Though he is less belligerent and unconcerned with the restorative power of traditional working-class experience, the emotional and political architecture of Nick Hornby's novels is perfectly compatible with these masculinist obsessions. His respecification of the limits of Englishness also depends upon being the right kind of man. In order to become themselves, his male characters award custodianship of meaningful human emotion exclusively to African Americans musicians like the great singers Solomon Burke and Al Green, who effectively speak for these post-Feminist boys-about-town in their confused dealings with the women they desire and upon whom their futures depend.

These writers are not the only Briterati who affirm post-Feminist responses to the country's changing structures of class, gender, and family and try to place their own wounded masculinity on the coveted throne of victimhood. Many more share a basic hope that the destructive processes that corrode family life from within can be reversed either by large dollops of masculinist nostalgia for a simpler, ordered working-class existence or by the reconstitution of the bourgeois household.

Devolution and disintegration have intensified the nagging uncertainty as to the cultural content of national identity that these writers try to fill with reconditioned masculinity. Is Britain's culture now morris dancing or line dancing? Are we in Gosford Park, Finsbury Park, or the park and ride? The failure to just know or, rather, to just feel what the nation's favored cultural filling should now be feeds the multicultural opportunity and the melancholic outlook. The latter gets compounded by the shrinkage of the national community and the disturbing news that the newly devolved partner nations in Scotland and Wales are evidently having a better time than the English. Their student grants have been restored, and their senior citizens will enjoy residential care without the indignities of means testing. The idea of England can no longer to be employed as a synonym for Britain and must contract to fit the diminished ideological space between political devolution based on alternative ethnicity and economic regionalization.

The discourse of imperiled Englishness is called upon to manage the stressful consequences of the great and growing split between city and country. Despite all its cosmopolitan diversity, London is in film and fiction likely to be purged of anyone who isn't white in what we can call "the Notting Hill effect."

In contrast, the breathless, elated multiculturalism of shows like *Changing Rooms* and *Ground Force* (unnoted by their critics in government) formalizes the delicate cultural operations involved in holding the elements of a new England together by manipulating its innermost private spaces and, in the process, showing that taste and lifestyle preference are much more important elements of identity than ethnicity, class, or regional ties could ever be. The liberating ordinariness that makes strangeness recede in a fog of paint fumes and sawdust must be weighed against the way that these programs furnish a guide to the limited areas of life that are amenable to change. By exploring the process of changing private space and refining the ability to act there, these shows offer an implicit justification of the refusal to act elsewhere. They dramatize the line between the space of legitimate agency and the stubborn aspects of social and political life that are untouchable, immutable, and resistant. The most fundamental message of this type of broadcasting is surely that, as far as the public world is concerned, there is no alternative.

Here too, the signature of melancholia can be seen. The insecure and perennially anxious nation revealed by these cultural discrepancies is inured to a variety of disappointment, for which the dreadful denouements at the end of *Changing Rooms* provide an excellent training. The country is then baffled by the demand to adjust itself to the challenging presence of racially different people, and this confusion, in turn, magically encapsulates the other conflicts evident in this transitional moment. Intrusions by immigrants, incompatible blacks, and fascinating, threatening strangers have come to symbolize all the difficulties involved in the country's grudging modernization. Outside the goldfish bowl of the *Big Brother* house, where we learn to take pleasure in seeing what living with difference adds up to, the conflicts that result soon call the desirability of that unchosen multicultural destination into question.

Creative and negative thinking is needed to generate more complex and challenging narratives, which can be faithful to the everyday patterns of heterocultural metropolitan life by reducing the exaggerated dimensions of racial difference to a liberating ordinaryness. From this angle, "race" would become nothing special, a virtual reality given meaning only by the fact that racism endures. These overdue revisions remain remote. The crude, dualistic architecture of racial discourse stubbornly militates against their appearance. It has to be brought into the realm of government.

Given the extent of Britain's deepening economic and social divisions, it is perhaps surprising that the convivial metropolitan cultures of the country's young people are still a bulwark against the machinations of racial politics. This enduring quality of resistance among the young is no trivial matter. It is much more than an effect of multicultural consumerism and communicates something of the irrevocably changed conditions in which factors of identity and solidarity that derive from class, gender, sexuality, and region have made a strong sense of racial difference unthinkable to the point of absurdity. The fact that so many British youth have been delivered to a place, as Nitin Sawhney memorably put it, "beyond skin," communicates how much those critical formations have changed.[25] Electronic dance music, almost always without words, has been a dominant form during most of these years. Its technological base and its metropolitan conditions of existence have promoted a spontaneous and ordinary hybridity that has, as The Streets continually remind us, been alloyed with recreational drug use on an extraordinary scale.

Amidst "deep-seated urban decay,"[26] racism is still enacted, but it is largely devoid of any strong belief in integral races. The resulting "subcultures" have lost nearly all of their old political flavors. They have been partially annexed by corporate power and exported around the globe without anyone associated with either politics or government being able to appreciate their worth as political and economic assets.

Growing inequality makes recognition of common interests more difficult because people are actually becoming less alike in economic terms. Their evasive commonality gets confined instead to the domain of global geopolitics where the country's dwindling fund of prestige can be seen to be immediately at stake and where its seemingly slavish dependency upon the whims of the United States have become a major problem.

4   The Negative Dialectics of Conviviality

We have seen that for more than thirty-five years, Britain's politics of race has been dominated by the combination of its postimperial melancholia with several versions of race talk. This unstable mixture identified the social and political problems embodied in the invasive presence of immigrants and their kin as an intrusion, an alien wedge cutting in to the body of an unsuspecting nation. It has helped to keep the anti-Nazi war at the center of the nation's sense of itself, to turn postcolonial settlers back into immigrants long after immigration had been stopped, and to saturate recent talk of refugees and asylum seekers with telltale traces of racial discourse regardless of any attempts to place these discussions on a more wholesome, post-Powell footing. We have also learned that the country's traditional desire—born in response to earlier stages of alien settlement—to push immigrants and immigration outside has neatly dovetailed with the new mood that fixes the interpretation of September 2001's horrors (and their ongoing aftermath) as a clash of contending civilizations with mutually incompatible cultural systems. Whatever the demographics of pensions provision and negative population growth may communicate, there is a powerful warning here for would-be architects of a multicultural future. A cat born in a kipper box will nonetheless remain a cat. The presence of British and other EU citizens among the hooded and chained al-Qaida prisoners in Caribbean detention has confirmed this judgement and tied it into the explanatory power of civilizationism.

For many commentators on the attacks on New York and Washington, the caged and rights-less prisoners deserve their fate because they have reverted to alien cultural type. Ethnic absolutism comprehends their evil and their affiliation to fundamentalist Islam as neither a choice nor an act of will. It sees these outcomes as the result of their instinctive responses to the combined pressures of ethnohistory, divergent tradition, and biocultural or even genomic division. Politically, the detainees' perverse tenure of British citizenship becomes nothing more than a retroactive indictment of the United Kingdom's overly lax immigration control and nationality legislation in the past. A good many of them can, if it becomes politically expedient, be retrospectively stripped of the citizenship they have wrongfully acquired. They have been among us, but they were never actually of us. Their presence in the United Kingdom is likely to have been the illegitimate result of arranged marriages designed to circumvent immigration control. The real source of their treacherous choices is likely to remain a private, spiritual matter disconnected from the patterns of everyday life inside Britain. Their fundamentalism is no more or less alien than was their misguided introduction into this country in the first place. They are traitors because immigrants are doomed in perpetuity to be outsiders. Becoming an enemy terrorist only makes explicit what was already implicit in their tragic and marginal position. Irrespective of where they are born, even their children and grandchildren will never really belong.

This Powellite folk analysis has been taken up by some powerful intellectual and political advocates in the pages of joined-up, policy-oriented journals like *Prospect*. It has another timely virtue; it ensures that young Britons' enthusiasm for political Islam has nothing whatsoever to do with domestic relations or domestic racism, with British policing, British schooling, British prisons, or Britain's labor market. Before the attacks on New York, the summer 2001 rioting in Britain's northern industrial towns had been ventriloquized to communicate the same duplicitous and facile version of racialized truth. Then, the rioters rioted because they were alien. The proof of their alienness was the fact that they had rioted. I think that this alienation from Britain has different roots in home soil. That possibility requires new thinking about the challenge of administering a multicultural polity, about the operation of trust, respect, and recognition.

It has become necessary to take political discussions of citizenship, belonging, and nationality beyond the dual prescription of assimilation and immigration control: the leftover categories of the 1960s debate. Interestingly, neither Britain's politicians nor its media are prepared to acknowledge that almost two additional generations have passed since anybody sat down and tried to make sense of the politics of race as a matter of policy. That compression of time might also be understood as a symptom. It makes the immigrants always seem to be stuck in the present. Devoid of historicity, their immediate circumstances are invested with an incontrovertible priority. The most frequent political response to the profound and militant disenchantment found among these young British people is located in the litany of ever more elaborate loyalty pledges and the associated fantasy that obligatory language training will somehow solve their problems of belonging. Those measures will do nothing to address the conditions that produce routine disaffection and exceptional treachery alike. Whatever problems gave rise to the summer rioting of 2001, the inability to speak English was not among them. It is not, as quite a few lazy commentators have suggested, that the presence of immigrants corrodes the homogeneity and solidarity that are necessary to the cohesion of authentically social-democratic regimes but rather that, in their flight away from socialistic principles and welfare-state inclusiveness and toward privatization and market liberalism, these beleaguered regimes have produced strangers and aliens as the populist limit against which increasingly evasive national particularity can be seen, felt, measured, and then, if need be, negatively discharged. The raw material for that perilous exercise is not supplied by aging representatives of the incoming caste of settler-citizens but by the two succeeding generations of their locally born descendants. That group gets trapped in the vulnerable role of perpetual outsider, but their local sense of entitlement leaves them reluctant to make common cause against racism and xenophobia with more recently arrived refugees and asylum seekers. To do so would be to accede to the secondariness and marginality with which racism associates them.

All of these changes can be used to point to the enduring significance of "race" and racism and their historic place in the long and slow transformation of Britain, its changing relationships with itself, with Europe, with the United States, and the wider postcolonial world. If the country has been modernized in the years since 1945, we should be able to appreciate that some sort of shift in the political culture around "race" has been intrinsic to that reluctant and at times regressive modernization. Proclaiming equality of opportunity is now, for example, an uncontroversial feature of every anodyne corporate mission statement, but those routine declarations seem to have no impact upon the fact that inequality is increasing. We certainly get to see more black people in the dreamscape of advertising, on television, and on the sports field, though not in Parliament, the police service, or the judge's bench. Our righteous and cosmopolitan government has even instituted a day on which we are urged to remember and mourn the victims of the Nazi genocide as an aide to cultivating better anti-racist morals. Politicians who have been engaged in seeking new ways to communicate their bright-eyed multicultural decency are even occasionally prepared to weep a few strategic crocodile tears over the latest unanticipated manifestations of street-level racial hatred. However, the triumph over racism has not been brought forward as a measure of modernization or an indication of national progress. There is no governmental interest in the forms of conviviality and intermixture that appear to have evolved spontaneously and organically from the interventions of anti-racists and the ordinary multiculture of the postcolonial metropolis. Instead, the tempo of race talk increases if organized neo-Fascists and white supremacists start to stalk the streets or if they seem on the edge of making an electoral breakthrough into respectable political society. However, that telltale urgency fades away once the demonic figures are routinized. Their ideology of race hatred gets easily reduced to an eccentric and predictable if not always understandable feature of the postindustrial landscape. It is, after all, a reaction triggered by the noisy demands of immigrants themselves. Class-bound Britons have always found it easier to discover the problems of racial nationalism in the fascinating shaven-headed forms of the neo-Nazi, young and fit, than in the anonymous pin-striped indifference of those who might not profess their commitment to race hierarchy in public after dark but whose actions institutionalize it nonetheless.

For every courageous soul prepared to entertain the idea that racism does exist in Britain or to suggest that it is an entrenched problem worthy of sustained political consideration and moral reflection, there are likely to be at least two indignant voices raised in opposition. The first is often a liberal one. It says grandly that making "race" a matter of government amounts to a form of special treatment illegitimately accorded to undeserving intruders and transients. The second is usually a conservative one. It is premised on the notion that national, cultural, and racial identities supply the single homogenous and unchanging center of social life and moralized community. This opinion proclaims itself unsurprised that, several generations after the Trojan horse of new commonwealth immigration was first wheeled into England's clean, peaceful, unsuspecting streets, the latter-day descendants of those original invaders provocatively maintain the alien cultures of their ancestors. The misguided social experiment that brought them into Britain was always doomed to fail. Their unexpected arrival and unwanted settlement were catastrophic because they cheaply sacrificed the social and cultural cohesion necessary to the maintenance of mutual obligation and tolerance that distinguished British life and on which its welfare state depended.

Once this picture is updated by factoring in the impact of a neoliberal consumer culture that can glamorize racial difference, we can be misled by the fact that a few black and Asian Britons may benefit from the love of exotica that has arisen in response to the rigors of living with difference, of being with the Other. This confusion is compounded when we discover that exciting, unfamiliar cultures can be consumed in the absence of any face-to-face recognition or real-time negotiation with their actual creators. The intensified desire for what was formerly stigmatized and forbidden can also be interpreted as a part of the collapse of English cultural confidence that has fed the development of anxious and insecure local and national identities. Today's new hatreds arise less from supposedly reliable anthropological knowledge of the stable identity and predictable difference of the Other. Their novel sources lie in the problem of not being able to locate the Other's difference in the commonsense lexicon of alterity. Different people are still hated and feared, but the timely antipathy against them is nothing compared to the hatreds turned toward the greater menace of the half-different and the partially familiar. To have mixed is to have been party to a great civilizational betrayal. Any unsettling traces of the resulting hybridity must therefore be excised from the tidy, bleached-out zones of impossibly pure culture.

The idea that both of the men indicted as members of bin Laden's international terrorist conspiracy have had intimate and decidedly postcolonial connections with black London life now needs to be considered. The story of black European involvement in the geopolitical currents of the war on terror can be connected to the history of immigration and race politics in some deep and disturbing ways. Zacarias Moussaoui, "the twentieth hijacker" was routinely described as a French citizen of Moroccan ancestry, but he lived in London for nine years and completed his education at South Bank University in the seedy cosmopolitan shadow of the Elephant and Castle. His brother, Abd Samad Moussaoui, wrote a powerful biographical study of his sibling's religious and political formation. It linked Zacarias' vulnerability to the attractions of Wahhabism to an experience of "cultural uprooting," which, in his brother's eyes, defined that long period in London:

> Those young Muslims who headed for London knew nothing about British society. They found themselves in a foreign land not necessarily welcoming, a land where foreigners like them are tolerated as long as they don't stray too far from their community. Zacarias, as we have seen, is a French man who is not at ease with being French, and a Moroccan who can't even speak Arabic. Which community does he belong to? His malaise would definitely foster a sense of belonging to the group that took him in.[1]

The network that connected Moussaoui to Richard Reid, the hapless, gigantic "Shoebomber," encompassed other European cities—Paris, Brussels, and Amsterdam—as well as London. We know that, like Reid, Moussaoui worshiped at the Brixton mosque, which like its more famous northern counterpart in Finsbury Park, seems to have provided a key location where the routine frustrations of people made angry and miserable by the everyday effects of white supremacy and its petty humiliations could be connected to the special balm of a fundamentalist utopia.

Twenty years before, lost, damaged, and disoriented young men like Richard Reid and Zacarias Moussaoui might have found comfort and sustenance in a different political, philosophical, and cultural system. At that point, the last flickers of globalized Ethiopianism and Rastafari livity still plausibly combined indictments of imperialism with the restorative rhetoric of Black Power. The Rastafari were ascetic. They spoke the language of peace and love and manipulated the poetics of human rights and justice, though not in liberal accents. At the end of the Cold War, they held provocatively to the fundamental unity of humankind—something that could only be recovered and made inspirational if the destructive power of racism could be acknowledged and then repaired. Wars would continue until the color of skin was of no more significance than the color of eyes, but once the colonial countries of southern Africa were liberated, it was clear that Jah People would not be waging them. Babylon's internal contradictions and conflicts were sufficient to bring its walls down. The incidental damage done to black life and community had, of course, to be addressed, but their basic plan, if that is not too formal a word for this process, was to accept the inevitability of suffering and sit out the phase of oppression patiently, armed with the belief that right, justice, history, and God were all on their side.

The later 1980s and the 1990s saw the vernacular eschatology of the Caribbean basin succeeded by a much more self-consciously militant and militaristic approach to black solidarity. This political culture was the obvious product of the overdeveloped world. A hip-hop mentality that derived from the traumatic geography of American Apartheid and was addressed to those distinctive conditions of inequality and exclusion replaced Ethiopianist asceticism and humility with a culture of play and excess. Martin Luther King became Uncle Tom, while Malcolm X was recovered manhood. Under the corporate tutelage of Spike Lee and company, consumerism, hedonism, and gun play were no longer to be incompatible with the long-term goals of racial uplift. Bigger investments in the present were necessary because the slaves' traditional belief in a better life after this one had started to fade away with their Christianity. For many, this mainstreaming of black culture was a shift that tainted and compromised the very core of black resistance. From then on, America's Afro-Baptist pieties were interpreted as an inducement to surrender rather than an invitation to revolution. It was Islam rather than Christianity that would supply the patch of solid ground on which postmodern black nationalism could plant its over-sized ideological feet.

Willing to break the hold of American-centered thought but unable to turn entirely from its racial phantasmagoria, the austere and authoritarian versions of black nationalism peddled in black London's underground publications like Pascoe Sawyers's *Alarm* turned in two directions. Firstly, they moved toward America's own versions of pseudo-fundamentalist Islam and then, bizarrely, toward the corporate idiom of public relations, commerce, business, and management. Fantasies of racial national rebirth were lubricated by the opportunistic wisdom of figures like black America's self-styled "truth terrorist," Dr. Khalid Muhammad. A highly selective and partial appropriation of Islamic motifs assisted in developing strict communitarian responses to the nihilism of consumer culture and the despair of fratricidal and suicidal violence. However, this Islam was leavened with diverse occult and New Age themes. In recognizably Protestant fashion, it soon turned inward and helped the desire to remake the world take second place behind the obligation to remake oneself. Power was exercised in ever more narrow circuits: over one's own body, on the ball court or at the gym, and, above all, in the regulation of interpersonal conduct between men and women, between parents and children. Instituting the right forms of masculinity was critical to the survival of the race and to the elaboration of its biopolitical and economic interests in reformed family units. This had as much or more to do with reorganizing intergenerational relationships as with reversing the basic outcomes of the Feminist settlement that had transformed domestic life.

As its own family and household structures fall apart, America was initially thrilled and horrified to be told that John Walker Lindh, its very own treacherous wigger Talib, was a suburban hip-hopper from an affluent Californian family who was turned into a Muslim fanatic through overexposure to the prison-conversion autobiography of Malcolm X. The idea of contamination by blackness is an old script. The notion that black militancy initiated Walker Lindh's descent into irrationality aided his defense. It enveloped his image as a traitor with some extra layers of psychological confusion. With his primal identity on the line, Walker Lindh started to become intelligible especially once it was discovered that his father, Frank Lindh, had abandoned his marriage for another man. Walker's treasonable acts then became comprehensible within the rules of a corrupted family romance.

Richard Reid was the product of a different pathology, signaled, above all, by the fact that after his arrest nobody knew what or who he was and where he might have come from. His parents were also prominent in the media quest for an explanation of his conduct, but his less pampered life told an altogether different sort of tale, as deeply English as Walker's had been North American. This story resonated loudly with the fundamental message carried by all those tales of the wild antics of maimed mullahs active at the perimeter of the Arsenal and elsewhere. The horrific figures of Reid the lumbering shoebomber and Abu "Captain Hook" Hamza were used to manifest the basic, uncomfortable truth that British multiculturalism had failed. Reid's place in history had been assured not by his ideological commitments or his almost comical ineptitude but by the bizarre instruments of his failed martyrdom: the sophisticated training-shoe bombs that enclosed his gigantic and unnaturally smelly, clown-sized feet.

In the context of all the simplistic rubbish that was spouted about his racially mixed parentage, those iconic feet were made to bear the extra weight of nineteenth-century theories of hybrid vigor. Like his enormous body, they not only confirmed Reid's essential monstrosity but presented him as the cuckoo in the national nest, nourished by God-fearing Britain's misplaced goodwill only to repay kindness with violence and indifference. His trainer-weapons made a dismal announcement to a world more used to savoring the cool Britannic achievements of less menacing celebrity "half-castes" like Ms. Dynamite, Sade, Scary Spice, Jade Goody, and Ryan Giggs. They were pitched into a debate between those who see race mixing as a routine and essentially banal feature of contemporary British life and those, on the other side, who think of it as a misguided social experiment that usually ends in tragedy if not in catastrophic violence. The vivid tabloid accounts of the Reid family's fortunes over several generations supported the latter, default view of the relationship between "race" culture and social pathology. From that angle, the seeds of Richard's tragedy had been sown long before by Hubert Reid, his Jamaican grandfather who migrated to Britain immediately after the war. It is with the figures of Richard's estranged father, Robin Colvin Reid, a wretched specimen of the "tragic mulatto" type, seemingly plucked from the depths of Enoch Powell's worst nightmares, and his mother, Lesley Hughes, a white Englishwoman who attracted much sympathy by having made a mistake thirty odd years ago, that things got serious, and all the damage done to the country by postwar immigration became vividly apparent.

Mrs. Hughes had the presence of mind to divorce her black husband and flee from the city to the countryside. From her rural home, she looked with palpable horror toward the bad behavior of her long-lost child who, like Victor Frankenstein's hideous offspring, had chosen a path of destruction as his compensation for exile from kith and kin. Bravely resisting the pressure to make failed family life into the overall explanation of his son's treachery, Robin Reid offered an eloquent counteranalysis of both their blighted lives. The various effects of British racism were cited repeatedly as he tried to create an emotional and psychological context in which his son's strange choices might become comprehensible. London-born Robin's words were undermined by the knowledge that, like his son, he too had been a criminal. He revealed that he had spent many of his fifty-one years behind bars for numerous minor offences. Though he had managed to go straight for the last nine, his disreputable character was confirmed in the press by the fact that he had been living on state benefits during all of that time. All these details tied his personal tragedy to the contemporary social problems represented by his symbolic kin—the desperate asylum seekers—who stormed the Channel tunnel to try and reach England's promised land a few nights later.

Though acknowledging his failure as a father, Robin Reid refused to identify that as the key to his son's fate. He claimed the credit for introducing the boy to the Islamic faith, which he, just like Malcolm X, had discovered while in prison and used subsequently as an antidote to the racism that bounded and broke his hopes. Robin Reid said firmly that he found refuge from that same racism in the fraternal kinship provided to him by the Hells Angels, who, exactly like the Islamic brotherhood that had taken in his errant son, did not care about either race or color. The historic tension between the claims of communities we choose and those into which we are born has seldom been more starkly stated. Richard

Reid's trial in October 2002 was a brief affair. He was reported to have been "smirking" in the dock and then pleaded guilty with these words of confession before a court, the legitimacy of which he claimed not to recognize: "I'm a follower of Osama bin Laden. I am an enemy of your country and I don't care."

A counterpoint to Reid's case can be deduced from the emphatically postcolonial tale of another terrifying Muslim cleric, Sheik Abdullah el-Faisal. He was sentenced to nine years at the Old Bailey in March 2003 for soliciting nonspecific murder and for incitement to racial hatred on cassettes of his speeches, which were offered for sale. The first charge, of encouraging others to murder persons unknown, was brought under the archaic 1861 Offences Against the Person Act, a statute that had lain unused for more than a century. The severity of the sentence passed for the incitement offence contrasted sharply with the milder punishments meted out to the British nationalists who have also been occasionally prosecuted for the same crime. The thirty-nine year old el-Faisal was born in Jamaica and passed his early years there as an enthusiastic member of the Salvation Army before turning to Islam at the age of sixteen and then moving to Saudi Arabia, where he spent eight years studying. It was announced after his sentencing that, despite the fact that his wife and children are British citizens, he will be deported once his sentence has been served. In the autumn of 2003, the British government was reported to be exploring the possibility of building a new prison of its own on the Caribbean island in order to house the burdensome total of 2,800 Jamaican nationals held in British jails. Not far away, in Cuba, there are still some British nationals held without charge or trial in the U.S. Camp Delta at Guantanamo Bay. They are confined among a total of approximately 600 prisoners who at the time of writing held citizenship from more than forty countries. The regime at the camp has been harshly judged by the International Red Cross, which had access to the detainees and noted a worrying deterioration in their mental health, and the International Bar Association's task force on international terrorism, which found problems in the way that inmates were neither accorded rights under the Geneva convention as prisoners of war nor recognized as civilians under the domestic laws of the United States.

Perhaps there is some variety of healing historical symmetry in these symbolically charged attempts to repatriate the West's problems to tropical climes. It was in Cuba that concentration camps were first added to the political technologies of colonial modernity in an episode that ushered in the "American Century" we have just left. Cuba is next to Jamaica, the island from which el-Faisal, then known as Trevor Forrest, embarked on his journey into the embrace of Wahhabism and from which Richard Reid's grandfather had set out for England during the late 1940s, armed only with a British passport as proof of his dubious right to belong. Half a century later, Britain's jails are brimful with Richard Reids, and the unacknowledged effects of institutional racism have polluted the waters of its civic culture. Demonic images of Reid and his peers will doubtless help to erase the limited but positive contribution made by the Macpherson report, but any analysis that fails to take Europe's postcolonial conflicts into account will not be able to explain why young black Europeans might find fundamentalism attractive and why they would be willing to hitch their hopes for a just world without racism to the absurd engine of an Islamic revolution.

Blair, Brent, and Blunkett in the Pluriverse of Ali G

The fundamentalism shared by Reid, el-Faisal, Moussaoui, and the rest takes a dim view of the seductions of multicultural society and of the fact that in Britain "race" has become ordinary. Crossracial sex is now no more or less meaningful than multiracial football. White kids routinely speak patois and borrow strategically from Punjabi. Charismatic leaders born in Jamaica can become eloquent mouthpieces of political Islam, and the most celebrated member of the local chapter of the U.S. Nation of Islam can be a professional comedian who is known to become rather defensive when asked about the fact that his pursuit of purity allows him to have an "Asian" wife. Impervious to these obvious changes but anxious about how their unchecked cultural consequences play in the marginals and shires, New Labour's leaders have recently confirmed their detachment from the world the rest of us inhabit by speaking heavy-handedly about the mechanical transmission of English norms, the regimentation of national identity, and the necessity of assimilation. Large doses of Harry Potter—whose anachronistic class-bound world looks as though it could benefit from a good dose of mass economic immigration—may hold the line for a while, but desperate gestures cannot conceal the fact that the problematic of assimilation lost its grip on the postcolonial world long, long ago.

We have been waiting for a more sophisticated and political understanding of cultural change, influence, and adaptation that can defend and explain the spontaneous tolerance and openness evident in the underworld of Britain's convivial culture. Pending the belated arrival of that long-delayed intervention, postcolonial melancholia invites us to pass the time not by laughing at ourselves and our national plight but by laughing at immigrants and strangers and, in particular, finding distraction and respite in the uneven results of the country's incomplete transition to cultural diversity and plurality. The tabloid newspapers in particular feed this response. They run sniggery front-page pieces that chronicle the uncivilized misdeeds of asylum seekers, who, we are told, have not only been barbecuing the Queen's swans but have apparently feasted on the innocent flesh of stolen sea-side donkeys who never did anything worse than take holiday-making children for well-deserved beach rides. These frequent invitations to manage the stresses of multiculture through a laugh and a joke provide a key to understanding the success of Ali G during the late 1990s and earliest 2000s, when his provocative early performances offered a satirical Rorschach blot in which even the most neurotic scrutinizers of the national psyche could discover their fears and their hopes.

That shape-shifting Ali G was funny at all supplies the proof that Home Secretary Blunkett and his traditionalist brigade were trying to close the stable door of British culture after the piebald horses of intermixture had disappeared over the horizon. Ali arrived at the March 2002 gala premier of his new movie *Ali G Ina da House* wearing a royal crown and opulent stately robes. He was flanked by six young women, whose modesty had been ensured by the application of plastic cannabis leaves over their minimal bikinis. Ali explained to the cameras that he had invited Princes Charles, William, and Harry to this event but they had not been able to attend "because Harry still owes me 20 pounds for an eighth." Christopher Tookey, the *Daily Mail*'s film critic, pronounced the movie to be the "laziest and most obnoxious British film" ever made. He continued: "the film resembles a collection of half-baked sketches assembled by someone with attention deficit syndrome. The impression is of a man cynically determined to cater for the scum of the earth, and make his humour as ugly, loutish and revolting as possible." It was entirely fitting that *Ali G Ina da House* won the distinction of being slammed by the *Mail*. Their critic's portentous denunciation was made primarily on grounds of taste. His view of Ali G as stupid and vulgar confirmed that he had missed the point entirely and simply did not understand the density and complexity with which the film's Rabelaisian idiom addressed the widening fissures in Britain's public culture.

Protesters from what used to be the opposite end of the political spectrum condemned the film and picketed its opening for different reasons. They accused Ali G's creator, Sacha Baron Cohen, of being a new Al Jolson, of exploiting black culture and pimping it into the media mainstream where he, rather than the community to which that culture really belonged, could turn a profit. The ideas of cultural ownership and experiential copyright on which that criticism depends are anachronistic, but the resort to them tells us a lot about contemporary anxieties over the integrity of marginal identity and the fluctuating value of minority culture. Ali G had fastened on to these problems and tried to make them both funny and productive of better racial politics. However, the gag was likely to be lost on those who felt that if they did not maintain an insider's monopoly on public use of ethnic code words like "*punany,*" the boundaries of their particularity could be compromised and their wounded identities would fall apart. Once again, the effects of racism bring out the worst in everybody. For those angry people, the betrayal that Ali G represented was the culmination of a larger process of dilution and mongrelization in which the protective purity of largely racial cultures was being lost, leaving them vulnerable to unprotected encounters with difference that can only involve risk, fear, and jeopardy.

If the film celebrated anything, it was the tedium of suburban life and the ethnic traditions of "Carry On" humor that correspond to it. Ali was not homophobic, macho, aggressive, or antisocial. He obeyed the speed limit, believed in the healing power of God's green herb, and had identified the terminal duplicity of all forms of politricks. He was loyal, decent, and honest. When punched by Charles Dance's repellent deputy prime minister, his response is to cry. These admirable qualities were entirely lost on the positive-image school of cultural critique, which has recently been getting into a lather over the antisocial antics of those real life Ali Gs, the So Solid Crew. Their South London adaptation of the U.S. gangsta moves is a surely symptom rather than a cause of inner-city chaos and gun play, but it fed the latest panic over black culture and yielded an unhelpful analysis of how deviant cultures and identities were being formed and reproduced. This commonsense view was so simplistic that it presented role models and mentors as the best answer to the ubiquitous failure of black boys who do badly at school not because of racism but because their teachers are afraid of them and their fathers are absent from their unhappy homes. This was the setting in which the panic over mugging reappeared and the destruction of our once-great nation was confirmed by the appearance of senior police officers who not only smoked ganja but subverted the proper order of things by refusing to arrest others for doing so.

It is significant that the central unifying joke underpinning all Ali G's work is supplied by an antipathy toward the stultifying U.S. styles and habits that have all but crushed local forms of the black vernacular and replaced them with the standardized and uniform global products of hip-hop consumer culture. Likeable Ali G shows that the globally broadcast

American thug life is ridiculously inappropriate to the more innocent habits of marginal young Brits. He makes the commitment to ghetto fabulous tastes and behaviors appear absurd. He is telling Britain that it had better find another way to go. This element of Ali's performances survived his transition to the big screen and remained evident even after he fell victim to what we can call the "Beavis and Butthead" syndrome: a condition of mass popularity in which any original satirical intentions are misrecognized as an affirmation of the object or process they try to subvert or ridicule.

No matter how ignorant, idiotic, and inept Ali G became, there were hordes of illiterate juveniles and pathetic hedonists ready to hail him as their hero: two parts Candide to one part Homer Simpson and one part Peter Sellers. If that ambiguity had been all there was to Ali's act, his appeal would not have lasted as long as it did. We cannot afford to overlook the other angles from which his translation jokes became funny, shuttling between different, discrepant versions of emergent multicultural England. Ali's original interviews with celebrities, experts, and politicians have to be triangulated. Apart from the place occupied by his idiotic inquiries and the position of the person being duped by him, there was always a third location from which the viewers, slyly guided by his wise foolishness, could move across cultural codes and between linguistic games. There, where a word like "caned" had acquired new meanings along antagonistic intergenerational lines, we could accept an invitation to become literate, if not exactly fluent, in irreversibly plural British culture. Popular celebrations of the stupid rather than the sly Ali G as a hero may have eventually defeated this enterprise, but they were a consequence of the character's subtleties as well as endearing traits like his carnivalesque contempt for the pompous and powerful people he was able to ambush, manipulate, and even humiliate in the interview segments of his TV shows.

The character of Ali G should be understood as a subtle reply to the fact that the influential pages of publications like *Prospect* and *The Salisbury Review* were groaning under the weight of speculations about the pathological characteristics of black culture, "black on black" violence, and, worse still, the transmission of antisocial alien mentalities into the urban dregs of wretched white, working-class life. If we accept Ali as his feature film presented him, that is, as a young white Briton, we can appreciate him as a comment upon as well as an ambassador from the emergent, multicultural Britain that exists, largely unnoticed and always unvalued, alongside its better-known, official counterpart. The hostile reactions against Ali G from right and left were also important, especially because their common source lay in anxiety about what he was and a radical uncertainty about what he might be. Zygmunt Bauman has called this sort of reaction to the unclassifiable "proteophobia." Just as with Richard Reid, no one knew for certain what Ali G was. Hatred, fear, and anxiety appeared in response to his ability to confound the racial and ethnic categories that held contemporary Britain stable. This was less an issue of his biology or phenotype than of his cultural mutability. The final destination of those proteophobic anxieties was uncertain, but they should matter in any conclusive evaluation of Ali G. After all, if he was not in fact pretending to be black then he could be absolved of the most serious charges of cultural theft and exploitation, which would make it easier to judge him on the basis of whether he can make us laugh without making us feel guilty in doing so.

It would be ridiculous to pretend that none of the people who found Ali G funny were laughing at him for the wrong reasons. Some would have been laughing at what they took to be his imitation or ridicule of blackness, others at one further remove, were probably laughing at the black parts of his monstrous hybrid. They could do this safely because they knew perfectly well that he was not really black. Nonetheless, their laughter existed far beyond the reach of any simplistic suggestion that it could be contained by its origins in a racist point of view. This incomplete inventory does not exhaust the possible sources of that laughter, but I have no doubt that many people would also have been laughing at what Ali G showed us about British culture. They laughed louder and longer because he revealed it to be alien, eccentric, and absurd in its snobbery, stupidity, and perverse attachment to numerous forms of destructive hierarchy—class, race, religion. Those dismal qualities were not being exposed from the outside by a stranger but explored from the inside in a daring act of patriotic love. By imagining himself as a stranger in his own country, Ali G refined a systematic estrangement from local habits and turned it into an art. Thus an undecidable Ali G remains preferable to the obvious retreat involved in making him into a joker in some New Labour pack of Britain's ethnic happy families. That unfixed and unstable Ali might also have helped to break laughter's complicity with postcolonial melancholia and to locate new sources of comedy in a remade relationship with our heterogeneous selves, working through the aftereffects of empire in a self-consciously multicultural nation. That laughter does not intersperse loathing and self-hatred with manic elation. It helps instead to cultivate the everyday, ordinary virtue involved in managing healthier relationships with otherness that are not deformed by fear, anxiety, and violence.

If these speculations sound farfetched, similar arguments can be considered in relation to the popularity of another comedy that succeeded

Britain's wave of Ali G mania. This was *The Office*, a spoof reality TV show, or "mockumentary," that examined the office culture of Wernham Hogg, a paper merchants in Slough, in the downbeat style of fly-on-the-wall programs like *Airport* and *Hotel*. *The Office* offered a distorted-mirror microcosm of Tony Blair's Britain in a peculiar collection of working people whose very ordinariness supplied the magic element that drew us into their narrow, suburban orbit and celebrated the country's slow but profound adaptation to the new tempo of its multicultural life. All of old Britain's obsessions, with class, race, gender, tradition, national identity, and even with the propriety of laughter itself were present here. *The Office* acknowledged them and then dramatized and celebrated their still incomplete overcoming. This was done in a complex dramatic process that made it difficult to dismiss the ambiguities of humor in simultaneously accommodating people to their discomfort in the world as it is while strengthening their ability to withstand the things they dislike about it and helping them to resist the intrusions of power and boredom into their irrepressible but precarious and alienated humanity. My fundamental point is that here, too, the complicity of laughter with Britain's postcolonial melancholia was explicitly identified and then broken.

The country's time-worn habit of dealing with racism through the ritual activity of having a laugh was dealt with directly in one extraordinary episode of *The Office* in which David Brent, the principal character, who is both office manager and a would-be comedian, gets rebuked for telling a racist joke in the presence of a black colleague and is then exposed to the lucid objections of his fellow workers who found it offensive. The joke in question will have offended monarchists as well as anti-racists by suggesting that the members of the royal family were intimately familiar with a "black man's cock." More importantly, it was drained of its meaning by the repeated retellings that this post-modern scenario required.

The Office was also notable for being the one vital, dynamic place in all of British culture where the language and practice of managerialism were held up to ridicule and the routinization of insecure employment was judged to be immoral and unjust. Apart from that, the program's conspicuous successes derived largely from its ability to turn an anthropological eye on the everyday workings of contemporary British social life and to make that exploratory journey into the interior of darkest England a source of insight, pleasure, and amusement. This pioneering operation was folded so as to include a satirically driven challenge to the ways in which reality was being constructed and projected by the codes of reality television.

In episode 5 of the first series, we follow the disenchanted office workers as they embark on an alcohol-fuelled trip to "Chasers," their local disco-pub. Their typically drab night out includes plenty of bawdy talk, and, as the episode concludes against the depressing backdrop of their empty pleasures framed by dead public space, the manager-comedian David Brent defends the integrity of contemporary working-class life and leisure against the contemptuous commentary he has discovered in John Betjeman's famous prewar poem, "Slough," which opens with the immortal line "Come friendly bombs and fall on Slough." To interpret this scene we need to remember that Brent is a devious and pathetic but hardly malevolent man. He sees himself not just as a great boss and dazzling business leader but as a "chilled-out comedian" and musician who is basically unworthy of the world of commerce to which he remains fiercely loyal mostly because it allows him to remain perpetually idle and never challenges his narcissism. Brent's weaknesses, in particular his vanity and absolute lack of principle, make him into a representative character who, incidentally, captures all the inconsistencies and shallowness of the New Labour project. His inability to comprehend the poem's view of Britain sets up an important joke with several layers that illuminates not only the core of *The Office* but the heart of the nation that recognized itself there. It is firstly a joke about England and Englishness, a joke about the nation's changing class and culture, about the oscillation between town and country, about the claims, pitfalls, and pleasures of incomplete modernization. This becomes a joke about the war because the poem sounds as though it was written after the Blitz, as an odd request for another, more liberating round of mass destruction rained down from above. Characteristically, Brent has misread Betjeman, interpreting his prewar words as if they belonged to the postwar period and linking them to the destruction of Coventry and the opportunities for town planning that it created. The office manager's commentary on the poem is not funny because we, the viewers, agree with Betjeman's portrait of the town. We do, however, marvel at the poet's prescient ability to have captured the Slough we have glimpsed through the interaction of the workers at Wernham Hogg. Betjeman seems to have anticipated the appearance of men like Brent when he denounces Slough's many clerks with these sinister lines:

> And get the man with double chin
> Who'll always cheat and always win,
> Who washes his repulsive skin
> In women's tears.

Brent responds to these parts of poem with a question that is worthy of Ali G: "What's the matter, doesn't he like girls?" Betjeman's antimodern view of Britain is held up to ridicule in the same gesture that allows our dislikes of Brent and of Slough to find expression. Our sense of the poem's mix of insight and absurdity is not the same as David Brent's. We can agree with much of his repudiation of Betjeman as "overated," old, and out of touch. We recoil from poet laureate's snobbery and what New Labour ideologues would identify as his "elitism." Brent's own hostility and perplexity confirm our sense that Betjeman's view is anachronistic. But Brent's defense of Slough is hyperbolic. It is even worse than Betjeman's critical commentary on the place and becomes funnier because of its class accent and petty, audibly Thatcherite tone. We have already become accustomed to the fact that Slough is far worse than Betjeman could ever have dreamed. That awfulness supplied the premise of *The Office*. Brent's cheery attachment to Slough confirms our sense of where we differ from him. His appreciation of Slough is of a piece with his cheap managerialism, his sleazy sexism, his casual racism, his selfishness, and his horribly patronizing approach to anybody who uses a wheelchair or is not, as he sees it, exactly like him.

War is at the center of Betjeman's interwar poem. It is kept at the center of *The Office* by the constant revelations about mundane experience in the character-building world of the Territorial Army, which flow from the absurdly militaristic imagination of Brent's lickspittle, Gareth Keenan. He is a man who, like many of his countrymen, enjoys watching *The Dambusters* on DVD because it fuels his postmodern patriotism, but in front of the camera crew, Gareth feels embarrassed that the dog in the movie is called "Nigger," something that he and Brent agree could only have happened "before racism was bad." Betjeman's imaginary bombs were "friendly" because unlike the Nazi munitions that would soon accomplish far less creative acts of destruction, they were reversing the historical direction of Britain's postwar modernization. *The Office* tacitly reveals that process to have been completed. Britain's multiculture has, in effect, detached London from England, thereby isolating the small-minded Englishness of lonely, damaged men like Brent and Gareth who think they have the full measure of the country's transformation but have utterly failed to grasp what it requires of them. Brent's reading of Betjeman's poem asks the viewer to consider what will now become of English nationalism in its suburban enclaves? Perhaps, because of this great change, the capital will have to shift outward down the M4, passing Ali G's Staines on its way westward. Slough could then become the new capital of a mediocre but more modest country that no longer knows its limits or the distinctive shape of its postcolonial social life as it desperately tries to invent a new "ethnic" content for its changed culture.

John Betjeman saw the only future for new English places like Slough as a forced return to their natural state. No immigrants complicated his dislike for these locations by making their upwardly mobile inhabitants—the hated clerks and their peroxide-haired wives—into victims of treacherous government. His joke was that Slough should be readied for the plow and the production of cabbages. David Brent's updated contribution is that, in line with Johnny Rotten's accurate predictions, he cannot see any future at all beyond the rising tide of management-speak and the sad, half-healing rituals of booze, quiz-night, conference, and consultancy that ready the e-mail proletariat for its next day at work.

Europe and Convivial Culture

Britain's politics of race ceases to be funny when the future it projects for the country derives entirely from U.S. scripts and statecraft. This is equally true whether the imported motifs are good—the civil rights movement—or bad—the Ku Klux Klan and its various offshoots. Even disguised by his classical analogies, it was obvious that the Powellite view of the future made American-style race war into the country's inevitable destination. I want to conclude by considering that problem and exploring some alternative scenarios for the nation's multicultural future. Some of these alternative directions are suggested when routine features of vernacular conviviality enter into the mainstream of British culture. The appearance of Aesat Selassie and Ita Barica, two Rastafarian "peace officers" from Handsworth, Birmingham, at the 2003 Conservative Party Conference was an event that, as we've already seen, can be easily counterpointed by things that take place in the consumer cultures of sport and music. Though neither of these emissaries from the inner city belonged to the Conservative Party or had ever voted for it, they had been invited to participate in the conference by breakfasting with Ian Duncan Smith and, in the process, contributing a dynamic image of Conservative inclusiveness and hospitality as they stood holding hands with his wife Betsy. At that very moment, research into the operation of the discretionary powers under section 60 of the Crime, Justice, and Public Order Act (1994) had shown that people of Caribbean descent or appearance were twenty-seven times more likely to be stopped and searched by the police than were white people. The second, historical fact does not undo or even reduce the obvious ambiguities of the first. We must first reestablish the historical setting in which melancholia has appeared to orchestrate their coming together.

In the mid 1950s, Aimé Césaire examined the condition of Europe, which was then in the grip of anticolonial conflicts and the aftershock of World War II. He pronounced a grim and memorable judgment. European civilization was decadent and dying. In failing to answer the reasonable demands made by its colonial peoples for liberation, it had proved incapable of justifying itself, either in terms of reason or in terms of conscience. He argued that this compound failure revealed European civilization to be incapable of solving the two major problems to which its modern existence had given rise: the problem of the proletariat and the colonial problem.[2]

Our judgment may be less categorical than this. It must necessarily be more alive to the ludic, cosmopolitan energy and the democratic possibilities so evident in the postcolonial metropolis. However, it is true that the big issue that we should address in order to evaluate the health of Europe's cultural and political institutions has arisen right at the intersection of the problems to which Césaire directed attention. Race and class have been articulated together, and profound questions concerning the depth and character of European democracy and unity are being posed by nationalist and racist responses to the claims of old settlers, new migrants, refugees, and asylum seekers. The traditional list of aliens has been recently supplemented by the addition of other shadowy, infrahuman figures: bodies without rights or recognition detained exceptionally in the course of the ongoing "war against terror." Few of these vulnerable people are postcolonial settlers. New inflow from those quarters had been shut out long ago. Simple exclusionary mechanisms have ensured that Europe's twenty-first-century retirement benefits will be paid for by Argentineans, Poles, and Slovaks rather than Nigerians, Jamaicans, and Somalis. Happily, in some places, the grandchildren of the 1950s settler-citizens are successfully negotiating their right to belong to European nations. Not all of the latest incomers are actively racialized, though many are, of course, demonized as Islamic terrorists in waiting.

My conclusions in this book depend upon a consideration of what the supposedly intrusive presence of strangers and the correspondingly punitive treatment dished out to them by various governments now suggests about the condition of European civilization and the British contribution to its understanding of multiculture. Europe stands today militarized once again and heavily fortified against its proliferating enemies, within and without. The war against asylum seekers, refugees, and economic migrants offers a chance to consider not just changing patterns of governmentality, commerce, and labor but to examine the changing cultural and ethical contours of Europe, where the notion of public good and the practice of politics seem to be in irreversible decline—undone by a combination of consumer culture, privatization, and the neoliberal ideology.

This breakdown can be used to show where the facile assumptions of civilizationism become untenable. It is also necessary to affirm that the peculiar synonymy of the terms "European" and "white" cannot continue. And yet, against a wealth of detailed historical and cultural evidence taken from all across Europe, identity, belonging, and, consequently, the imperiled integrity of national states are being communicated through the language and symbols of absolute ethnicity and *racialized* difference. This mixture of ethnicity and identity was identified long ago as essential to the workings of culturalist racism, which succeeded the cruder, biological varieties in the second half of the twentieth century.[3] Two practical consequences follow: Firstly, that historians of Europe's repressed, denied, and disavowed blackness must become willing to say the same things over and over again in the hope that a climate will eventually develop in which we will be able to find a hearing, and, secondly, that we must be prepared to step back audaciously into the past. This should be done not just to establish where the boundaries of the post-colonial present should fall but also to enlist Europe's largely untapped heterological and imperial histories in the urgent service of contemporary multiculture and future pluralism. The little-known historical facts of Europe's openness to the colonial worlds it helped to make must be employed to challenge fantasies of the newly embattled European region as a culturally bleached or politically fortified space, closed off to further immigration, barred to asylum seeking and willfully deaf to any demand for hospitality made by refugees and other displaced people.

My argument has associated the midcentury mass migration of formerly colonial peoples to Europe with the cultural turn in race thinking. That old "new racism" exerts an influence even as it fades and cedes its dubious authority to emergent genomic and biosocial explanations. Its distinctive anthropological tones are still audible in the subtleties and evasions characteristic of the racializing discourse to which "culture talk"[4] gives enduring expression. Europe's commonsense racism now articulates the language of cultural difference blandly and fluently. Even the Islamophobic belligerence of the post–September 11 environment is not usually inclined to be overt. The crudest expressions of racial antipathy are still redolent of imperial and colonial domination. The denial, guilt, and shame induced by melancholia mean that such obvious distaste is usually regarded as unsavory, indiscrete, disreputable, and offensive. But the underlying cultural codes remain alive. They have been buried inside anodyne forms of nationalism and patriotism that are seldom judged harshly, at least when viewed from above. Those varieties of solidarity are actually welcomed as desirable features of social and political life. It is thought that they endow national communities with a necessary strength and a positive confidence. Under those populist banners, which have become far more important since official politics became boring and the idea of public good fell into disrepute, the standard of what counts as acceptable commentary has been sharply altered. Arranged reverently around national flagpoles, the mean-spirited people who only a short time before sounded like unreconstructed nativists, racists, ultranationalists, and neo-Fascists turn out instead to be postmodern patriots and anxious, pragmatic liberals eager to be insulated from the chill of globalization by the warm glow of cosmopolitan imperialism, bolstered by newly invented cultural homogeneity.

Defending the simple hierarchies engineered during the nineteenth century is no longer the principal concern. Instead, emphasis falls on the wider dimensions of cultural and, thanks to Huntington and company, civilizational difference. Those divisions are just as intractable and fundamental as the natural hierarchies they have partly replaced, but they have acquired extra moral credibility and additional political authority by being closer to respectable and realistic cultural nationalism and more remote from bio-logic of any kind. As a result, we are informed not only that the mutually exclusive cultures of indigenes and incomers cannot be compatible but also that mistaken attempts to mix or even dwell peaceably together can bring only destruction.[5] From this perspective, exposure to otherness is always going to be risky. Contact with aliens feeds uncertainty and promotes ontological jeopardy. Predictably, the resulting dangers are acute for those with the most to lose in a tumble from the giddy heights of their natural and cultural superiority. These themes have now supplied the staple content for European racial nationalisms all the way from Sweden to Rome.[6]

At the same time, the feral beauty of postcolonial culture, literature, and art of all kinds is already contributing to the making of new European cultures. That development can be used to complicate any oversimple picture of resurgent neo-Fascism and ultranationalism, but the arts alone cannot provide an antidote to the problems that make culture and ethnicity so widely and automatically resonant. Something bolder and more imaginative is called for. We need to be able to see how the presence of strangers, aliens, and blacks and the distinctive dynamics of Europe's imperial history have combined to shape its cultural and political habits and institutions. These historical processes have to be understood as internal to the operations of European political culture. They do not represent the constitutive outside of Europe's modern and modernist life. They can be shown to be alive in the interior spaces and mechanisms through which Europe has come to know and interpret itself, to define its passions, paths, and habits in opposition to the U.S. models that are identified with an inevitable future of racial conflict.

Most polite, mainstream interests recoil in horror from the prospect of colonial history providing an opening onto the multicultural promise of the postcolonial world. Distaste is registered in the anthropological tongue and then moves without apparent effort through the sham wisdom of incommensurable cultural difference, contending civilizations, opposed religions, and untranslatable customs. Those *volkish* themes are anxious emanations from a brittle culture that, following Césaire's midcentury diagnosis, is in deep denial about the global dimensions of its imperial history and the compromised morality of its colonial historicity. Contemporary culture talk is comfortably contained by the idiom of populist racism, with its litany of hatred against bogus asylum seekers, aggressive beggars, and devious thieves—the latest vectors of danger, dirt, disease, and crime. It bears repetition that, however archly innocent they may strive to be, the patterning of these thoughts associates them with the oldest xenophobic impulses.

Europe's congested metropolitan spaces stage puzzling confrontations with unblinking alien alterity. The strange, threatening groups in question turn out to be the very ones that were already well known and firmly fixed under the sign of race. The old hierarchies produced by race thinking's excursions into political anatomy are recycled and endorsed for the test of absolute culture that they provide. In other words, culture talk draws renewed power from the specifications of racial difference that are smuggled inside it. Critics and historians of this period must become more alert to the oblique connections that have made Europe's cultural history into a battleground. If it is to be intellectually as well as politically productive, critical work must be ready to confront imperial denial and the flourishing revisionist scholarship that supports it. Effective opposition to racism, nationalism, and ethnic absolutism must be able to resignify the complicated discursive figures that have made tacitly race-coded common sense an attractive option for confused and anxious European folk and for their increasingly cynical and manipulative political leaders as both groups confront the perils and opportunities of globalization.[7]

The wider ethical climate in which, for Europe, fervent governmental or popular racism can be made to hark back to the Third Reich must also surely be taken into account. But as the history of that genocidal conflict is also being mystified and forgotten, the corrective power of shame at complicity cannot be relied upon to supply or renew limited ethical resources.

It bears repetition that the biopolitical commitments, which were previously mandated by old-style racial hierarchy, persist in the form of common sense even after the languages of absolute cultural difference and genetic determinism start to take hold. The residual traces of imperial racism combine easily with mechanistic notions of culture and a deterministic organicism to form a deadly cocktail. These operations are no longer being exclusively conducted by the neo-Fascists and the ultra-Right. They have also been attractive to the aspirations of the social-democratic Left. Indeed, the populist metaphysics of "race," nation, and identity fudges those increasingly fluid categories.

Once the fears of the host community, rather than racism, are identified as a substantive object of government and statecraft, race will have acquired the power to reconfigure the political field by revealing unforeseen connections that operate across the formal divisions of ideology and party. These developments are clearly visible through the prisms provided in Britain by politically motivated counterhistories of race, racism, and culture. The critical study of those formations can help to generate a new, anti-racist cartography of Europe addressed to the quality and character of the continent's postcolonial predicament.

The convenient argument that some cultural differences are so profound that they cannot be bridged has become commonplace. It can be explained by the way that nationality gets blurred once "race" has becomes a matter of culture. That absence of clarity is telling. It suggests that anyone who makes a fuss about racism, past or present, is getting things out of proportion, engaging in witch-hunts, practicing empty moralism, or indulging in the immature outlooks of "loony leftism" and, above all, "political correctness." From this perspective, the conceptual and semantic interconnections that have been established between the forms of language that produce "race," "nation," and "culture" as interchangeable, rather than networked terms are ruled irrelevant.

Because "race" *ought* (according to the tenets of liberalism) to be nothing, it *is* prematurely pronounced to be of no consequence whatsoever. Racism either disappears at this point or lingers on as a marginal issue, an essentially prepolitical event that should not be addressed by any government worthy of the name. To even suggest that it might be worthwhile to approach racism politically threatens a debasement of government and a travesty of justice. There is, in fact, no substantive problem here because racism requires no specific intervention beyond the worn-out rubrics of generic liberalism. Any fool knows that real, grown-up, joined-up governments cannot legislate the emotions of their populations. We are warned that any attempt to do so inclines them toward totalitarianism.

Arrayed against that type of argument is another disabling script. It bears the deep imprint of conditions and struggles over race and racism in North America. This orientation answers the liberal culture of denial by saying that "race" is not nothing but everything: a permanent and apparently inescapable feature of society. This avowedly radical assertion is not a tactical response to the complacent voices that regularly deny the most obvious manifestations of racial division and hierarchy. This position does not aim to promote recognition of the unstable potency of racism in economic, social, and political relations. It is more concerned with arguing that any aspiration to live outside of racialized bonds, codes, and structures of feeling is naïve, misplaced, foolish, or devious. It insists rightly that there is a racial ordering of the world, that we must comprehend it historically and endeavor to represent it analytically with an epistemological valence and scholarly rigor comparable to those more usually found in critical projects centered on class and gender. But before taking a stand against the patience required by bringing race into politics, this approach turns instead toward fatalism and resignation. It is noteworthy that this U.S.-centric discourse is animated not by a confrontation with racism(s) or even racialized hierarchy but by its extreme attachments to a reified notion of race. Race becomes above all an experiential and therapeutic question that identifies a zone of feeling and being that is considered to be emphatically prior to all merely political considerations. In this setting, a totemic concept of race is present but abstract. Sometimes it specifies visible differences lodged in or discovered on and around the body, but this attention to what can be seen does not exhaust it. In other moments, race becomes a signifier for generic problems of cultural plurality and translation.

Neither of these depressing but popular options is satisfactory. The first is complacent and essentially indifferent to the sufferings of those whose lives are still conditioned by western imperial and colonial power. The second is equally unsatisfying because it refuses the prospect of race as politics and opts instead to stay comfortably inside the safer areas where critical analysis is unnecessary and narcissistic expressions of feeling will always be sufficient. As far as the articulation of race with culture is concerned, these warring positions or tendencies are equally comfortable with absolutist notions of cultural particularity and diversity. That shared focus is put to diametrically opposed political uses.

These positions can only be answered by exploring the detailed unfolding of cultural formations. The aim of this is not to construct a history of simple hybridity to offset against the achievements of the homogenizers and purity seekers. Instead, local and specific interventions can contribute to a counterhistory of cultural relations and influences from which a new understanding of multicultural Europe will doubtless eventually emerge. This negative work can discover and explore some of the emancipatory possibilities that are implicitly at stake in convivial culture but do not announce themselves, preferring to remain hidden and unpredictable. This choice is aligned with the ordinary, spontaneous antiracism that has also emerged intermittently. Its small triumphs bring real pleasure, but they can evaporate and count for little once invasive immigration has been constructed as an intractable problem with national dimensions.

At that point, hybrid urban cultures and cosmopolitan, creolized history go out of the window. Instead we get transported into the frozen realm of mythic time that has been shaped around the master analogy of immigration as a form of warfare. That unhappy, archaic domain is populated by the timeless, iconic ciphers of postcolonial melancholia: criminals, spongers, and their numberless alien offspring. Their presence manifests a racial order, which presents the problematic diversity that black settlers and strangers have inserted into Europe's political bodies as an effect of their simple, unchanging alien ways. Complexity, on the other hand, like history and indeed like the evolutionary momentum of development itself, is the apparent monopoly of those who are in possession of the precious solidarity that derives from cultural unanimity.

Justifying their pessimistic responses to the nightmare of looming multiculture leads policy makers to opine that it is "easier to feel solidarity with those who broadly share your values and way of life,"[8] as if the assimilation of interwar Germany's Jews provided an obstacle rather than an incentive to their murder. If that strand of European history offers any insights into the present moment, which can be characterized by resurgent ultranationalism and neo-Fascism, it might suggest that much of the time, the anger and hatred that racisms promote can be triggered even by modest success in attempts at sharing "values and way of life" across the leaky barriers of race and absolute ethnicity.

Anti-racists are now obliged to judge where acceptable national feeling ends and xenophobic racism commences. We must find new courage to reflect on the history of political nationalism that has been entangled with the ideas of race, culture, and civilization and to understand how Europe's imperial and colonial dominance brought racisms and nationalisms together in ways that still affect present conditions. The hard work of postcolonial culture building encompasses several additional confrontations: The first of these is aimed at the realization of a more worthwhile liberalism. This variant might, for example, prepare to be profaned by systematic reflections upon its own colonial habits and implications.[9] It might also be able to confront the impulses which specify racial, ethnic, and national divisions in subtle patterns that are as potent as they are inferential. The second conflict involves an assault upon the pragmatic formulae that place both racism and antiracism outside of the political field, leaving them to be essentially private issues, matters of taste, preference, and, ultimately, of consumer or lifestyle choice. A third confrontation would perhaps culminate in a revised account of European modernisms and their complex relationship with colonial and imperial experiences at home and abroad. A fourth would be directed toward understanding the impact of black literature, culture, art, and music on European life, and in particular seeing how during the latter half of the twentieth century an appetite for various African American cultures was part of how Europe recomposed itself in the aftermath of Fascism.

These interpretative puzzles have been rendered more difficult to solve because the ground on which the ramshackle edifice of political antiracism was erected—largely, we should remember, by incomers and their supporters—has dwindled. That notable contribution to Europe's civic well-being and political health passes unremarked upon by those who babble instead about the endless conflict between local solidarity and alien diversity. Hasn't antiracism demanded more solid and supple forms of democracy? Couldn't a dynamic and worthwhile solidarity be articulated around the noble desire for racism to have no place in Europe's democratic political cultures?

Anyway, with hybrid culture on our side and postcolonial counterhistory at our disposal, antiracism should move out of its defensive and apologetic postures. Its aims are now being annexed by corporate interests that are a good deal less squeamish than governments about feeding the popular hunger for a world purged of racial conflicts. However, the market-driven pastiche of multiculture that is manipulated from above by commerce only appears compelling and attractive in the absence of governmental action and political initiatives organized from below.[10] Most corporate attempts at ventriloquizing the desire to live lives that are not amenable to race coding have been ham-fisted. The betrayal of that utopia is obvious where racial types are reinscribed in the service of commercial reach rather than abolished in the name of human freedom. Meanwhile, the nonracial ideal is more likely to be at risk of being rendered banal by the carnival of heteroculture now at large in the metropolis.

As the implications of these large changes begin to dawn, we should acknowledge that the routinization of that cultural plurality does not mean that the work of antiracism is over. That project must go on because the wholesome, democratic cadences of nonracial nationalism are not being heard either as loudly or as frequently as their advocates had anticipated they would be. In many instances, it would appear that the mere presence of new "waves" of immigrants is enough to silence the cheerleaders of tolerance, negative or positive. Faced with this degree of inertia, another battle ensues that requires us to be alert to the workings of political racism and able to apprehend "race" as a process of relation, imaginary kinship, and real narration rather than some badge worn on or lodged deep inside the body. Without making any concessions to the reification of "race" and ethnic identity, we must try to find ways to take the divisive dehumanizing power of race thinking more seriously than in the past. In other words, we must be prepared to identify racism as a specific and significant object, to comprehend it as a part of a web of discourse, to see that it has a knowable history, and to appreciate its social implication in the exercise of the biopolitical powers that have damaged European democracy before and can still compromise it. Taking racist discourse and cultural intermixture that seriously involves scholarly as well as political tasks. It demonstrates that there can be no excuses for failure to become intimate with the history of Europe's modern invention and projection of humanity in racially divided, antagonistic, and hierarchical encampments. A command of that contested domestic history is all the more important as the living memory of the Third Reich dies out and ceases to form the constellation under which critical, oppositional, reflexive work can take place. The automatic assumption that European history will be told best and most powerfully when it is made to coincide with the fixed borders of its national states will also have to be disposed of.

In drawing the new map of Britain in Europe that we will need to accomplish these tasks, we must be prepared to make detours into the imperial and colonial zones where the catastrophic power of race thinking was first institutionalized and its distinctive anthropologies first put to the test, above all, in the civilizing storms of colonial war. Making that long-forgotten history coextensive with the moral lives of European nations is essential, but a viable antiracism cannot end with the sense of shame that story ought to produce. That redemptive movement must be able to pass beyond a compensatory acknowledgment of Europe's imperial crimes and the significance of its colonies as places of governmental innovation and experiment. The empires were not simply out there—distant terminal points for trading activity where race consciousness could grow—in the torrid zones of the world at the other end of the colonial chain. Imperial mentalities were brought back home long before the immigrants arrived and altered economic, social, and cultural relations in the core of Europe's colonial systems. This shift in standpoint makes those imperial dynamics much more significant in the constitution of national states than they have been allowed to be before. It sets a number of challenges before historians of the postcolonial present.

We have seen that the principled opposition to nationalism that was so important to Socialist and Feminist traditions has faded away with the ashes of the Cold War. Scholastic orthodoxy is now keen to reinterpret the xenophobia, nationalism, and ethnic absolutism of today's racists in benign ways. If their hateful responses are not immediately intelligible as a grumbling anticapitalism, then they must be heard as a new anxiety, something induced by the experience of deindustrialization or by the fear of downward mobility and the growing inequality that has been prompted by turbo-capitalism's merciless destruction of once-proud welfare states.

We have already heard some scholastic voices argue that racism is not a substantive issue for Europe's future. Others add that culturalist and nationalist racism is not proper racism after all but rather a veiled protest against the rupture of Europe's post-1945 settlement by unwanted mass immigration. The either-or-ism of these shallow explanations is deeply problematic. A more useful approach would seek to understand why it is through the political language of race that these destabilizing statements of dissent and fear become expressible.

Faced with strangers seeking entry to Europe's fortress, today's civic and ethnic nationalisms reply negatively in one hostile voice. If we are to situate, interpret, and then answer that uniform rejection, we must be careful about returning to what we can call a "migrancy problematic." The mistaken choice involved in centering work on migration introduces a risk of collusion with the cheap consensus that ties immigration and social policy to the nebulous discussions of diversity, multiculturalism and "political correctness" that I have already criticized. The figure of the immigrant is part of the very intellectual mechanism that holds us—as postcolonial Europeans, black and white, indeterminate and unclassifiable—hostage. Its prominence returns our discourse, against our will, to the idea that immigration and its discontents contain the key to understanding all the bids for recognition, belonging, and autonomy that have been made recently by the original incomers and their locally born descendants. This should not mean, of course, that the history of migration is to be abandoned before it has even been produced. It means instead that fascination with the figure of the migrant must be made part of Europe's history rather than its contemporary geography. The postcolonial migrant needs to be recognized as an anachronistic figure bound to the lost imperial past. We need to conjure up a future in which black and brown Europeans stop being seen as migrants. Migration becomes doubly unhelpful when it alone supplies an explanation for the conflicts and opportunities of this transitional moment in the life of Europe's polities, economies, and cultural ensembles. I prefer to say that if there has to be one single concept, a solitary unifying idea around which the history of postcolonial settlement in twentieth-century Europe should revolve, that place of glory should be given not to migrancy but to racism. The racisms of Europe's colonial and imperial phase preceded the appearance of migrants inside the European citadel. It was racism and not diversity that made their arrival into a problem. This is more than just a question of perspective. There are significant political interests at stake. Where migrancy supplies the decisive element, the door gets opened to patterns of explanation that ultimately present immigrants as the authors of their own misfortune. The violence and hostility regularly directed against them by their reluctant hosts can then be excused. That depressed and depressing view must be answered with a different kind of analysis, to which mutable, itinerant culture is central. This approach is premised upon a commitment to make modern racism part of the moral landscape through which today's political processes must move.

The outrages, deaths, and dogged campaigns of resistance and recognition so evident during the recent years have created just enough hope to sustain a fragile belief that a restored and healthier Britain might one day teach the rest of Europe something about what will have to be done in order to live peacefully with difference, to manage the hatreds directed against postcolonial and sanctuary-seeking peoples, and to contain the murderous mischief of organized neo-Nazis, ultranationalists, and other racist groups. This hope suggests that there are other stories about "race" and racism to be told apart from the endless narrative of immigration as invasion and the melancholic blend of guilt, denial, laughter, and homogenizing violence that it has precipitated. Those emancipatory interruptions can perhaps be defined by a liberating sense of the banality of intermixture and the subversive ordinariness of this country's convivial cultures in which "race" is stripped of meaning and racism, as it fades, becomes only an aftereffect of long-gone imperial history rather than a sign of Europe's North American destiny.

Aside from its parochial obligations to the rebirth of English tolerance and generosity, I hope it has been clear that this line of argument is also intended to be a modest contribution to the making of the planetary humanism discussed earlier. The newness of that mentality resides precisely in the ways that it is systematically opened to the difficult work of understanding of how "race thinking" configured and distorted the exclusionary humanisms of the past. That detour through modern histories of suffering must be made mandatory. It provides an invaluable means to locate ethical and political principles that can guide the work of building more just and equitable social relations. This is not antiracism of the type that says we must learn to love and value human differences rather than fear and misrecognize them. It is a new project because it is prepared to break with the notion that racial differences are a self-evident, immutable fact of political life. It refuses the idea that that this order of difference is somehow necessary to the very stability of our conflicted world. Instead, it suggests that the reification of race must be challenged if effective work against racism is to be accomplished. It seeks to turn the tables on all purity seekers, whoever they may be, to force them to account for their phobia about otherness and their violent hostility in the face of the clanging, self-evident sameness of suffering humankind. The version of multiculturalism that takes shape at this point is not then a lifestyle option. Its dissident value is confirmed everywhere in the chaotic pleasures of the convivial postcolonial urban world.

These arguments are marked by the desire to make it as easy for people to imagine a world without racial differences as it is for them currently to imagine the end of the world. The commitment to being recognized as a black European proclaimed here is hopefully part of a larger transition that may take us beyond racialized and racializable categories of all kinds. If it is currently impossible to acquire or even imagine that variety of "postethnic" European identity, that state of affairs is not only a result of the racism that still blocks the paths toward belonging but of the enduring power of racial identities as such. The abortive discussions that began at the 2001 Durban conference on racism and other forms of inequality and shut down prematurely in the aftermath of the terrorist attacks on New York and Washington may yet prove to be the beginning of a truly global opportunity to grasp the damage that "race" and racism have done to democracy and to hope alike. We do not know where this planetary conversation will take us or even whether the concept of racism will ultimately be an adequate vehicle for the cosmopolitan histories of hierarchy and inequality we will need. Historical analyses of racial hierarchy that overflow the fading boundaries of national states are essential to the credibility of that adventurous project. The recent history of Britain shows that it does not lag behind the United States in racial politics but has embarked on an altogether different path toward the goal of multicultural democracy. The lessons that have been learned and the pleasures that have been found along that route have not been brought into politics or government. I hope it does not sound melodramatic to say that the future of Europe depends upon what can now be made of that legacy.

Notes

Introduction. On Living with Difference

1. J. C. Flugel, "Tolerance," in *Psychoanalysis and Culture*, ed. George B. Wilbur and Warner Muensterberger (1951; reprint, New York: Wiley and Sons, 1967), 196–217.

2. Niall Ferguson, *Empire: The Rise and Demise of the British World Order and the Lessons for Global Power* (New York: Basic Books, 2002); Saul David, *The Indian Mutiny* (New York: Penguin Books, 2002).

3. This concept was developed in Renato Rosaldo, *Culture and Truth: The Re-Making of Social Analysis* (Boston: Beacon Press, 1989).

4. See *The National Security Strategy of the United states of America* (Falls Village, Conn.: Winterhouse Editions, 2002). See also Nicholas Lehmann, "The

Next World Order," *The New Yorker*, 1 April 2002, 45–48, which includes this illuminating quote from Richard Haass: "What you're seeing from the Administration is the emergence of a new principle or body of ideas—I'm not sure it constitutes a doctrine—about what you might call the limits of sovereignty. Sovereignty entails obligations. One is not to massacre your own people. Another is not to support terrorism in any way. If a government fails to meet these obligations, then it forfeits some of the normal advantages of sovereignty, including the right to be left alone inside your own territory. Other governments, including the United States, gain the right to intervene. In the case of terrorism, this can even lead to a right of preventive, or peremptory, self-defense. You essentially can act in anticipation if you have grounds to think it's a question of when, and not if, you're going to be attacked" (47).

5. Immanuel Kant, *Observations on the Feeling of the Beautiful and the Sublime*, trans. John T. Goldthwait (Berkeley: University of California Press, 1960), section 4. See also Ronald A. T. Judy, *Dis-Forming The American Canon* (Minneapolis: University of Minnesota Press, 1993).

6. Enrique Dussel, *The Invention of the Americas*, trans. Michael D. Barber (New York: Continuum Books, 1995), 10.

7. The full text of this infamous memo, dated 12 December 1991, is preserved at www.counterpunch.org/summers.html. See also Allan Chase, *The Legacy of Malthus: The Social Costs of the New Scientific Racism* (New York: Knopf, 1977), especially chapter 16.

8. This is a term taken from W. E. B. DuBois. The phrase *"tertium quid"* occurs in his much reprinted 1903 text, *The Souls of Black Folk*.

9. Michael Ignatieff, "Less Race, Please" *Prospect*, April 1999, 10.

10. Michael Ignatieff, *The Rights Revolution* (Toronto: House of Anansi Press, 2000), 115.

11. Jean-Paul Sartre, *Anti-Semite and Jew: An Exploration of the Etiology of Hate*, trans. Goerge J. Becker (New York: Schocken Books, 1948).

12. "Such is the lesson of history. It shows us that all civilisations derive from the white race, that none can exist without its help, and that a society is great and brilliant only so far as it preserves the blood of the noble group that created it, provided that this groups itself belongs to the most illustrious branch of our species." Arthur de Gobineau, *The Inequality of Human Races*, trans, Adrian Collins (1915; reprint, New York: Howard Fertig, 1999), 210.

13. Carl Schmitt, *The Concept of the Political*, trans. George Schwab (Chicago: University of Chicago Press, 1996), 54.

14. Schmitt, *The Concept of the Political*, 27–28.

15. Gad Heuman, *"The Killing Time": The Morant Bay Rebellion in Jamaica* (New York: Macmillan Books, 1994).

16. Leon Radzinowicz, *A History of English Criminal Law*, vol. 4 (London: Stevens and Sons, 1968), 143–52.

17. Colonel C. E. Callwell, *Small Wars: Their Principle and Practice* (1899; reprint, Lincoln, Neb.: Bison Books 1996), 219.

18. George Orwell, "Not Counting The Niggers," *The Adelphi*, July 1939.

19. Gobineau, *The Inequality of Human Races*, 211. Schmitt could be intro-

duced here as a mediating presence between the figures of Gobineau and Huntington. He too is concerned with the issue of homogeneity in *The Concept of The Political.*

20. Samuel P. Huntington, *The Clash of Civilizations and the Remaking of World Order* (New York: Simon and Schuster, 1997), 318.

21. George Orwell, "Notes On Nationalism," in *Orwell and Politics* (Harmondsworth: Penguin Books, 2001), 374.

22. David Jones, "Apartheid Britain," *Daily Mirror*, 23 June 2001.

1. Race and the Right to Be Human

1. T. W. Adorno "The Essay As Form," in *Notes to Literature*, trans. Sherry Weber Nicholson, vol. 1 (New York: Columbia University Press, 1991) , 4.

2. W. E. B. DuBois, *The World and Africa* (New York: Viking, 1947), 1.

3. Zygmunt Bauman, *Life in Fragments: Essays in Postmodern Morality* (Oxford: Blackwell, 1995), chapter 7.

4. W. E. B. DuBois, *The Crisis*, December 1910, 107.

5. Malcolm X with Alex Haley, *The Autobiography of Malcolm X* (New York: Penguin Books, 1965), 274–75.

6. Frantz Fanon, *Toward the African Revolution*, trans. Haakon Chevalier (New York: Monthly Review Press, 1967), 44.

7. Fanon, *Toward the African Revolution*, 18.

8. Ian Hacking "Making Up People," in *Reconstructing Individualism: Autonomy, Individuality, and the Self in Western Thought*, ed. Thomas C. Heller et al. (Stanford, Calif.: Stanford University Press, 1986)222–36. Working in a distinctive problematic shaped by the work of Jacques Derrida, Stuart Hall has expressed the same point from a rather different angle: "This is not the binary form of difference, between what is absolutely the same, and what is absolutely 'Other.' It is a 'weave' of similarities and differences that refuse to separate into fixed binary oppositions." Stuart Hall, "Conclusion: The Multi-Cultural Question," in *Un/settled Multiculturalisms: Diasporas, Entanglements*, ed. Barnor Hesse (London: Zed Press, 2000), 216.

9. Michael Ignatieff, "It's War but It Doesn't Have to Be Dirty" *Guardian*, 1 October 2001, http://www.guardian.co.uk/Archive/Article/0,4273,4267406,00.html.

10. Two examples suffice here. First, on the invention and application of fingerprint technology in India, see Chandak Sengoopta, *Imprint of The Raj: How Fingerprinting Was Born in Colonial India* (New York: Macmillan, 2003); The second is the circulation of Frank Kitson's doctrines for fighting "Low Intensity Warfare." These ideas and techniques traveled from Kenya to Ireland, Ireland to England. See Roger Faligot, *Britain's Military Strategy in Ireland: The Kitson Experiment* (London: Zed Press, 1983).

11. Sir Garnett Wolseley, "The Negro As a Soldier," *The Fortnightly Review*, no. 264, 1 December 1888.

12. Kenneth Ballhatchet, *Race, Sex, and Class Under the Raj: Imperial Attitudes and Policies and Their Critics* (London: Weidenfeld and Nicolson, 1980).

13. Jean Fouchard, *The Haitian Maroons: Liberty or Death*, trans. A Faulkner Watts, New York: Blyden Press, 1981), especially chapter 7.

14. Jon M. Bridgman, *The Revolt of the Hereros* (Berkeley: University of California Press, 1981); Clive Turnbull, *Black War: The Extermination of the Tasmanian Aborigines* (Melbourne: F. W. Cheshire, 1948).

15. Enrique Dussel, *The Invention of the Americas*, trans. Michael D. Barber (New York: Continuum, 1995).

16. Dorinda Outram, *The Body in the French Revolution: Sex, Class, and Political Culture* (New Haven, Conn.: Yale University Press, 1989); Peter Linebaugh, *The London Hanged: Crime and Civil Society in the Eighteenth Century* (Harmondsworth: Penguin Books, 1991).

17. Peter Fryer, *Black People in the British Empire: An Introduction* (London: Pluto Press, 1988), 110.

18. R. M. Coopland, *A Lady's Escape from Gwalior and Life in the Fort of Agra During the Mutinies of 1857* (London: Smith, Elder and Co., 1859), 233.

19. Henry Melville, *The History of the Island of Van Diemen's Land from the Year 1824 to 1825 Inclusive* (London: Smith and Elder, 1835), quoted in Clive Turnbull, *Black War*, 97.

20. Dee Brown, *Bury My Heart at Wounded Knee: An Indian History of the American West* (London: Pan Books, 1972), 72.

21. Roger Casement, "The Congo Report," in *The Black Diaries*, ed. Peter Singleton-Gates and Maurice Girodias (Paris: Olympia Press, 1959) 144.

22. Giorgio Agamben, *Homo Sacer: Sovereign Power and Bare Life* (Stanford, CAlif.: Stanford University Press, 1998).

23. Richard H. Grove, *Ecology, Climate, and Empire: Colonialism and Global Environmental History, 1400–1940* (Cambridge: White Horse Press, 1997), especially chapter 1; Michael Taussig, *Shamanism, Colonialsm, and the Wild Man: A Study in Terror and Healing* (Chicago: University of Chicago Press, 1987), especially chapter 3.

24. John M. Kaye FRS, *A History of the Sepoy War in India*, vol. 2 (London: W. H. Allen, 1881), 397–400, affords an insightful discussion of General Neill's judicial strategies for the punishment of "mutineers" at Cawnpore. See also pages 236–37 for a vivid account of the operation of martial law during the same period.

25. John McKenzie, *Propaganda and Empire* (Manchester: University of Manchester Press, 1986); E. M. Spiers "The Use of the Dum Dum Bullet in Colonial Warfare," *Journal of Imperial and Commonwealth History* 4, no. 1 (October 1975): 3–14. Wolseley, "The Negro As a Soldier."

26. Uday Singh Mehta, *Liberalism and Empire: A Study in Nineteenth-Century British Social Thought* (Chicago: University of Chicago Press, 1999).

27. Stan Cohen, *States of Denial* (Cambridge: Polity, 2001).

28. Karl Löwith, "The Occasional Decisionism of Carl Schmitt," in *Martin Heidegger and European Nihilism*, trans. Gary Steiner, ed. Richard Wolin (New York: Columbia University Press, 1995), 154.

29. Frantz Fanon, *The Wretched of the Earth*, trans. Constance Farrington (New York: Penguin Books, 1967), 116.

2. Cosmopolitanism Contested

1. *The National Security Strategy of the United States of America* (Falls Village, Conn.: Winterhouse Editions, 2002).

2. E. Banning, *L'Afrique et la conference geographique de Bruxelles* (Brussels, 1878), 123–24.

3. Banning, *L'Afrique et la conference geographique de Bruxelles*, 184–88.

4. Joseph Chamberlain, *Mr. Chamberlain's Speeches*, ed. Charles W. Boyd (London: Constable, 1914), 2–5.

5. Trevor Kavanagh, "Prepare To Fight," *The Sun* (London), 11 October 2001.

6. Sigmund Freud, *Civilization and Its Discontents*, trans. Joan Riviere, ed. James Strachey (London: Hogarth Press, 1963), 39.

7. Claude Lévi-Strauss, "Race and History," in *The Race Question in Modern Science*, ed. UNESCO (London: Sidgwick and Jackson, 1956), 129, 158.

8. Sigmund Freud, "Thoughts for the Times on War and Death," part 1, "The Disillusionment of the War," in *The Standard Edition of the Complete Psychological Works*, trans. and ed. James Strachey et al., vol. 14, 1914–16 (London: The Hogarth Press, 1957), 279–80.

9. Adrienne Rich, "Disloyal to Civilization," in *On Lies, Secrets, and Silence: Selected Prose, 1966–1978* (New York: Norton, 1979), 310.

10. Hannah Arendt, *Origins of Totalitarianism*, 3rd ed. (New York: Harcourt Brace, 1967), 124.

11. Carl Schmitt, *Land and Sea*, trans. Simona Draghici (Washington, D.C.: Plutarch Press), 37; Denis Cosgrove, *Apollo's Eye* (Baltimore: Johns Hopkins University Press), 2001.

12. Giacomo Leopardi, *Pensieri*, trans. W. S. Di Piero (Baton Rouge: Louisiana State University Press, 1981), 111.

13. George Orwell, "Shooting an Elephant," in *Orwell and Politics: Animal Farm in the Context of Essays, Reviews, and Letters Selected from* The Complete Works of George Orwell, ed. Peter Davison (Hramondsworh: Penguin, 2001), 22.

14. George Orwell, "Not Counting the Niggers," in *Orwell and Politics*, 69.

15. Jocelyn Hurndall, interview, *Evening Standard* (London), 16 July 2003.

16. See http://www.haaretz.com/hasen/pages/ShArt.jhtml?itemNo=312010&sw=%27Rachel+Corrie%27.

17. Rachel Corrie to her mother, 27 February 2003, http://www.guardian.co.uk/Print/0,3858,4627222,00.html.

18. Chris McGreal, "Activist's Memorial Service Disrupted," *The Guardian*, 19 March 2003.

19. This new imperialism is to be a joint UK–U.S. initiative, in opposition to the United Nations. It's primary spokesman is Robert Cooper. See his *Reordering the World: The Long Term Implications of September 11* (London: Foreign Policy Centre, 2002) and *The Postmodern State and the World Order* (London: Demos, 2000). In "The Next Empire," *Prospect* October 2001, he had this to say about past and future empires: "The weak states of the post-imperial world are disastrous for those who live in them and are bad for the rest of us. . . . The domino theory was false for communism but it may be true for chaos. . . . All the conditions seem to be there for a new imperialism. There are countries that need an outside force to

create stability . . . a system in which the strong protect the weak, in which the efficient and the well-governed export stability and liberty, in which the world is open for investment and growth—all of these seem eminently desirable. If empire has not often been like that, it has frequently been better than the chaos and barbarism that it replaced. There have even been times and places . . . where it has helped the spread of civilization" (24–25). He imagines that this new colonial rule will become "voluntary" and operate under the "lightest of touches."

3. "Has It Come to This?"

1. Cited in Paul Foot, *Immigration and Race in British Politics* (Harmondsworth: Penguin, 1965), 106.

2. Peter Kilfoyle, "With Friends Like These," *The Guardian*, 18 August 2003.

3. Linda Colley, *Captives: The Story of Britain's Pursuit of Empire and How Its Soldiers and Civilians Were Held Captive by the Dream of Global Supremacy, 1600–1850* (New York: Pantheon, 2002), 18.

4. Colley, *Captives*, 377.

5. For England is not flag or Empire it is not money and it is not blood
   it's limestone gorge and granite fell, it's Wealden clay and Severn mud,
   it's blackbird singing from the may tree, lark ascending through the scales
   it's robin watching from your spade and English earth beneath your nails.

This song, written by Maggie Holland appears on June Tabor's 2000 recording *A Quiet Eye* (Green Linnet).

6. These words come from the song "Turn the Page." The final line of this extract recalls the extraordinary scene in Orwell's *1984* when Winston and Julia come unexpectedly upon a thrush while out in the country. Skinner's description of the birdsong as lazy suggests not that his birds are unmotivated but that there is a radical purposelessness about the way they proceed. This insight was turned to different purpose by Orwell, who endows his thrush with the power to transform thought into feeling, with an ancient, almost pagan capacity to awaken the couple's sexual desire and, in Winston's mind at least, an arresting aesthetic force sufficient to confound any party functionary who could be spying on their secret liaison. "A thrush had alighted on a bough not five metres away, almost at the level of their faces. Perhaps it had not seen them. It was in the sun, they in the shade. It spread out its wings, fitted them carefully into place again, ducked its head for a moment, as though making a sort of obeisance to the sun, and then began to pour forth a torrent of song. In the afternoon hush the volume of the sound was startling. Winston and Julia clung together, fascinated. The music went on and on, minute after minute, with astonishing variations, never once repeating itself, almost as if the bird were deliberately showing off its virtuosity. Sometimes it stopped for a few seconds, spread out and resettled its wings, then swelled its speckled breast and again burst into song. Winston watched it with a sort of vague reverence. For whom, for what was that bird singing? No mate, no rival was watching it. What made it sit at the edge of the lonely wood and pour its music into nothingness? He wondered whether after all there was a microphone hidden somewhere near . . . it would pick up the thrush. Perhaps at the other end of the

instrument some small beetle-like man was listening intently—listening to *that*." George Orwell, *1984* (Harmondsworth: Penguin, 1968), 102.

7. Alexander and Margarete Mitscherlich, *The Inability to Mourn: Principles of Collective Behavior*, trans. Beverly R. Paczek (1967; reprint, New York: Grove Press, 1975), xx.

8. Quoted in Enoch Powell, *Freedom and Reality* (Surrey: Elliot Right Way Books, 1969), 282.

9. Matthew Tempest, "Blunkett: Refugees Should Rebuild Their Own Countries," *The Guardian*, 18 September 2002.

10. Anthony Giddens, "The Third Way Can Beat the Far Right," *The Guardian*, 3 May 2002.

11. Sir William Macpherson, *The Stephen Lawrence Inquiry: Report of an Inquiry by Sir William Macpherson of Cluny*, Cm 4262-1 (London: The Stationery Office, 1999).

12. Paul Barker, "Break This Murderous Fashion," *The Guardian*, 7 January 2003.

13. See, for example, the lurid coverage of the horrible assault on Norman and Cathy Green from Dorset, Terry Kirby, "Gang Stabs British Tourist on Remote South African Beach," *The Independent*, 27 November 2002. At one point, it was rumored that the Foreign Office had advised UK visitors to South Africa to take out "rape insurance."

14. Robert Cooper, *The Postmodern State and the World Order* (London: Demos, 2000), 39.

15. This text, which has attracted a lot of interest in the "post-9/11" climate, is published in English as *The Battle of the Casbah: Terrorism and Counter-Terrorism in Algeria, 1955–1957* (New York: Enigma Books, 2002).

16. Think, for example, of the lies that Blair told about his own childhood passion for Newcastle United and happy Saturday afternoons spent on the Gallowgate end of St James' Park and of his bestowing a knighthood on Geoff Hurst. An unqualified pledge to bring the games to Britain was included in Labour's 1997 election manifesto. See also Frank Keating, "Blair Learnt the Hard Way That Sport Can Bite Back," *The Guardian*, 27 May 2002.

17. Tyson was interviewed by Anthony Harwood. His compassion for Bruno also included a number of observations on Britain: "I love Brixton, just to drive around there sends shivers down my spine." Mike Tyson, interview by Anthony Harwood, *Daily Mirror* (London), 4 October 2003.

18. Jeremy Paxma, *The English: A Portrait of a People* (Harmondsworth: Penguin, 1999).

19. Peter Ackroyd, *Albion: The Origins of the English Imagination* (London: Chatto and Windus, 2002).

20. Roger Scruton, *England: An Elegy* (London: Chatto and Windus, 2000).

21. Roger Scruton, *England: An Elegy*, 4–7.

22. Stuart Hall, "Black Men, White Media," *Savacou* (Kingston, Jamaica) 9/10 (1974): 97–100.

23. George Orwell, "Notes on Nationalism," in *Orwell and Politics: Animal*

Farm *in the Context of Essays, Reviews, and Letters Selected from* The Complete Works of George Orwell, ed. Peter Davison (Hramondsworh: Penguin, 2001), 355.

24. Nick Hornby, *How to Be Good* (London: Viking, 2001).

25. Nitin Sawhney, *Beyond Skin*, Outcaste Records, CD, 1999.

26. The Streets, "Has It Come to This," from *Original Pirate Material*, Locked On Records, CD, 2002.

4. The Negative Dialectics of Conviviality

1. Abd Samad Moussaoui with Florence Bouquillat, *Zacarias Moussaoui: The Making of a Terrorist*, trans. Simon Pleasance and Fronza Woods (London: Serpent's Tail, 2003), 116.

2. Aimé Césaire, *Discourse on Colonialism*, trans. Joan Pinkham (New York: Monthly Review Press, 1972).

3. Martin Barker, *The New Racism* (London: Junction Books, 1981).

4. Mahmood Mamdani, ed., *Beyond Rights Talk and Culture Talk* (New York: St. Martins Press, 2000).

5. Bob Rowthorn, "In Defence of Fortress Europe," *Prospect* (February 2003)" 24–31; John Lloyd, "Poor Whites" *Prospect* (June 2002): 44–48.

6. Giles Tremlett, "Immigrant s Provoke Ire in Catalonia," *The Guardian*, 1 March 2001; Rory Carroll, "Italy Orders Anti-fascist Snatch Squads at Lazio," *The Guardian*, 2 February 2000.

7. At a rally in Paris, on May Day 2002, Jean-Marie Le Pen told his dwindling band of followers, "Globalisation and its Trojan horse, a federal Europe, are leading France to its death." John Hooper and JonHenley, "Eurpoe's Far Right Loses Its Way," *The Guardian*, 2 May 2002.

8. Alan Wolfe and Jytte Klausen, "Other People," *Prospect* (December 2000): 28–33.

9. James Tully, *Strange Multiplicity: Constitutionalism in an Age of Diversity* (Cambridge: Cambridge University Press, 1995).

10. Slavoj Žižek, "Multiculturalism, or, the Cultural Logic of Multinational Capitalism," *New Left Review* 225 (September/October 1997): 28–51.

Acknowledgments

This book is an expanded version of the Wellek Library Lectures given at University of California, Irvine, in the early summer of 2002. I am most grateful to everyone who was involved in that extended event. I am also indebted to people who argued with me at the other institutions where I tried to refine the arguments and try out some supplementary ones. Wits University in Johannesburg, The Institute of Education, London University; University of Rhode Island; State University of New York, Stonybrook; Istituto Universitario Orientale, Naples; Bard College; Tate Modern; and The New School.

In Irvine, I was especially grateful to Liisa Malkki for her warmth and kindness; to Lisa Ness, who makes an excellent cup of tea, to David Theo

Goldberg, who took time out from his surfing to get me to clarify the racial nomos; and Glen Mimura, who managed to persuade me that L.A. is changing for the better.

Away from Irvine, I want to thank my friends Ed Vulliamy, Paul Elliman, Hedvig Ekerwald, Les Back, Angela McRobbie, Achille Mbembe, Nikolas Rose, Vikki Bell, Jon Savage, Garry Younge, Donald Moore, Flemming Røgilds, St. Claire Bourne, Robert Young, Janet Giarratano, Geneva Melvin, Sarah Nuttall, and Anthony Barnett, for the conversations which are doubtless echoed here.

In my London life, I am grateful to Isaac Julien, Mark Nash, Fran Ware, Cath Ritchins, Stuart Hall, Brenda Kelly, Mandy Rose, Mark Ainley, Bridget Orr, and Bisi Williams for various forms of friendship, support, and fellowship.

I would like to thank my Yale colleagues, especially Alondra Nelson, Matt Jacobson, Hazel Carby, Michael Veal, Jeff Alexander, and Dan Friedman. I also thank my students, from whom I learn so much, especially Cassie Hays, Mary Barr, Lucia Trimbur, Louise Bernard, Radiclani Clytus, Robbie Sambat, Tavia Nyong'o, and Hiroki Ogasawara.

Steve Carr, Mark Baier, and Mark Sampson are thanked for their peerless command of what is now called vacuum-tube sonics—swords into ploughshares indeed. Gerard Melançon, Mean Gene Baker, Johan Gustavsson, and Paul Reed Smith are bigged up for knowing which pieces of wood are right, and Bob Peiper and George Youngblood recognized for helping me to take care of their extraordinary creations.

A shout out goes to Marcus Miller, Wayne Krantz, Jimmy Herring, and Gonzalo Rubalcaba in appreciation of some magical New York nights.

Cora Gilroy Ware was an acute and demanding guide to the maelstrom of popular culture and consumerism. Marcus Gilroy Ware kept me "on task" with his humane intelligence and indignation at the way our world is going. Last, but also always first, are my heartfelt thanks to Vron Ware, who has shared, cared, prompted, pressed, punctuated, stimulated, and inspired me for twenty-five years now. Without her, nothing.

Finsbury Park and Guilford, Connecticut

Index